D0627620

HUNGRIER FOR HEALTH

127 delicious, nutritious dishes
to help
prevent and reverse disease

Susan Silberstein, PhD

INFINITY
PUBLISHING

Copyright © 2011 by Susan Silberstein
Revised 2015 Edition

ISBN 978-0-7414-6434-7

Printed in the United States of America

Published August 2015

INFINITY PUBLISHING
1094 New DeHaven Street, Suite 100
West Conshohocken, PA 19428-2713
Toll-free (877) BUY BOOK
Local Phone (610) 941-9999
Fax (610) 941-9959
Info@buybooksontheweb.com
www.buybooksontheweb.com

In Praise of *Hungrier for Health*

"An edible platter of information delivered with authority, compassion, and humor. *Hungrier for Health* encourages all level students to ask more questions about our food and our health. The ingredients used in this book's mouthwatering recipes are champion supporters of health."
—Ana Negron, MD
Founder, GreensOnaBudget.org

"What a delicious solution to our current healthcare crisis! Patients I see who follow the wisdom in this book enjoy health and vitality far beyond that expected for their age."
--Todd Hoover. MD
President, American Institute of Homeopathy

"A truly fabulous collection of healthy recipes made simple and delicious. This book documents contemporary research that shows us how to live with awareness of what we are eating. It provides profoundly important nutrition information for every health seeker in America."
—Kathryn Boschert, MA, RD, LD
Past Director, Children's Research Foundation

"This is a wonderful book! …. Susan delivers a masterpiece from her heart, another proof of her long lasting commitment to healing people as only she can: with humor, wit, and solid data from which to draw serious conclusions. A true recipe for health, not only for individuals but for society. These wonderful recipes will help many of my patients in their road to improving life."
—Bernardo A. Merizalde, MD
Clinical Assistant Professor
Thomas Jefferson University

"What an excellent work – it is well-researched, user-friendly, and loaded with information that really needs to be gotten out."
— Mauris Emeka
Author, Cancer's Best Medicine

"This is absolutely wonderful: the content, the presentation, and the writing itself. I love this book! It will be a good friend to those looking to protect and improve their health, their future, and their families. I highly recommend *Hungrier for Health* for its delightful writing and its wisdom, based on modern advances in the sciences of cell biology and nutrition. Add to that the ancient wisdom of making things taste naturally good, and you have a great recipe for health and hope!"
—Candace Corson, MD
Board Certified Family Practitioner

"Dr. Silberstein has aced again. She cuts through the myths and fallacies, demystifying healthy plant food-based eating, and backs it up with easy to understand sound science. And the recipes are *to live for*: simple, easy to prepare, delicious, and *healthy*! This book is a real winner and a MUST for anyone who wants to achieve their best health ever!"
—Marilyn Joyce, PhD, RD
Former Director of Nutrition
Cancer Treatment Centers of America

To My Children

TABLE OF CONTENTS

Preface

Do NOT read this book! I mean it! If you have not read my first book, *Hungry for Health,* or its equivalent, and have not incorporated its four principles into your diet, don't even THINK about reading this one – especially if you have not given up diet soda and cheeseburgers. Trust me, you are not ready: You need to take Hungry for Health 101 first; this is the graduate course. If you are not eating primitive, colorful, alkaline and organic as a matter of course in your life, believe me you don't want to read *Hungrier for Health* – because now there is REALLY nothing to eat (just kidding)!

The recipes in *Hungrier for Health* are not only animal-free, they are also dairy-free, wheat-free, and gluten-free, and definitely microwave-free. But they are not only for vegetarians or vegans. It is my hope that non-vegans, lacto-ovo vegetarians, fish-eating vegetarians, and non-vegetarian animal eaters will adopt many of the delicious plants-only recipes in this book as healthful additions to the meals they are used to consuming, even if they are not intending to adhere to a strictly vegan diet. In fact, a vegan diet is actually inappropriate for certain metabolic types. Some people do not thrive on an all plant diet, especially if it is heavy in grains.

Why buy a recipe book these days when there are hundreds of thousands of recipes you can get online for free? Well, I started with those online recipes too. But what you see in this book is hardly ever how I downloaded it: Many recipes I found were unappealing to the taste buds, used difficult to find ingredients, were too complicated to execute, took too long to prepare, contained ingredients that were not vegan or gluten-free, and/or most importantly, included poor quality ingredients or cooking methods not in keeping with my health standards. So I changed nearly every single one! Moreover, often the recipes omitted the number of servings they produced or just gave ingredient guidelines without exact amounts. Right-brainers always cook that way; I, like most people trying to follow a recipe for the first time, am a left-brainer. If I make something I like, I want to know exactly what I did so I can duplicate it.

In my first recipe book, *Hungry for Health*, I tried to use as common ingredients as possible in my effort to prove that really tasty, healthful dishes can be simple to prepare with easy to find ingredients. In *Hungrier for Health*, I continue that mission of offering **simple, nutritious and delicious recipes**, but I also work with some less common and slightly more sophisticated – although not really exotic – ingredients.

These ingredients include natural sweeteners like Sucanat (dehydrated cane juice), stevia, and brown rice syrup; seeds like hemp seeds and chia seeds (salba); flours and starches like almond meal, tapioca flour, and arrowroot powder; grains like buckwheat soba and quinoa flakes; seasonings like Liquid Smoke, wheat-free tamari, and chili pepper sauce; and store-bought prepared ingredients like almond milk, coconut milk, coconut milk yogurt, and Daiya vegan "cheese."

As before, I recommend using the purest, highest quality, organic and unadulterated ingredients you can possibly find – including water.

I also follow the same format as in *Hungry for Health*, because people seem to really love the six categories, the nutrition quotes – all new – and the helpful hints, tasty tips, and nutri-notes. But this time I made the index more user-friendly by listing the recipes by their categories and by featuring main ingredients rather than just alphabetizing by the recipe name.

While this book is as natural, vegan and gluten-free as possible, it is not entirely raw -- a discipline which, although extremely healthful, is not somthing everyone can thrive on or adhere to perfectly in daily life.

I wish to express my special thanks first and foremost to **Natalie Dyen** for illustrating and formatting, to **Rachael Metz, Kathryn Turk, Dr. Jacquilen Fostor Tomas Ali, Sherry Milner**, and **Anthony Dissen** for contributing and testing recipes, to **Maria Fiorello** for researching nutrition notes, to my husband **Tony** and my dog **Butterscotch** — my official tasters, to all my *Hungry for Health* fans who sent letters of praise and encouraged me to write a sequel, and to all those extreme health-seekers who requested that the sequel be vegan.

It is my pleasure to donate profits from sales of this book to help support the wonderful work of
BeatCancer.org -- the Center for Advancement in Cancer Education, a national not-for-profit organization that specializes in dietary and lifestyle training for cancer prevention, prevention of recurrence, and support during or after treatment. For more information or additional copies of this book, contact:

Center for Advancement in Cancer Education
130 Almshouse Road #107
Richboro, PA 18954
www.BeatCancer.org
info@BeatCancer.org
888-551-2223

INTRODUCTION

The First Four Principles

Let's start with a quick review of the fundamental principles of healthy eating discussed in *Hungry for Health*.

Eat Primitive - For tens of thousand years, the human species consumed the hunter-gatherer society diet. Only since the Industrial Revolution brought modern food processing techniques has our diet changed so drastically that our cells can't recognize our food. Chronic killer diseases like cancer, heart disease and diabetes are the result.

Eat Colorful - The typical American diet is made up of white foods like milk, flour and sugar. We need to consume 13 daily servings of colorful fruits and vegetables, which contain up to 30,000 natural chemicals (phytonutrients), including 600 carotenes for immune system and antioxidant protection.

Eat Alkaline - On a scale of 0-14, where 0 is the most acid and 14 is the most alkaline, disease thrives in acidosis and healing takes place in alkalinity, when the blood pH is at least 7.3 or 7.4. Eating a ratio of 80% alkalinizing foods to 20% acidifying foods can increase energy, normalize weight, and protect against disease.

Eat Organic - Organic foods are not only better because of what is left out (pesticides, growth hormones and other chemical additives), but also because of what is left in (optimal levels of minerals, antioxidants, and other phytonutrients).

For those readers who have incorporated these first principles into their lives, we will now examine four more principles of healthy eating – principles that correlate with, explore in more depth, and build on the original four: Eat Natural, Eat Vegan, Eat Raw, and Eat Native.

1. Eat Natural

Natural — what a really vague term! The term has both multiple definitions and no definitions.

When I think of eating "natural" I think of eating foods as close to their natural state as possible – and sometimes that is on a continuum: an apple off an unsprayed tree is better than an apple off a truck; an apple off a truck is better than apple sauce; freshly made apple sauce is better than apple sauce in a jar; apple sauce in a jar is better than apple juice in a bottle, and definitely better than an "all natural" apple turnover with added high-fructose corn syrup!

Natural foods are generally assumed to be foods that are minimally processed and do not contain any hormones, antibiotics, colors or flavors that were not originally in the foods.

"Eat Natural" certainly sounds a lot like "Eat Primitive" and "Eat Organic," so why do we need another principle here? Let me explain.

Although there is an international standard for the term "organic" as established by the international Food and Agriculture Organization's *Codex Alimentarius,* there is no legal definition for the term "natural." Since almost all foods are processed in some way, either mechanically, chemically, or by temperature, it is difficult to define which type of food processing is really natural, and hence there are multiple definitions for "natural foods," while many countries offer no definition at all.

The Canadian Food Inspection Agency restricts the use of "natural" to foods that have not been significantly altered by processing. A natural food or ingredient of a food is one that does not have any constituent or fraction thereof removed or significantly changed, except the removal of water.

In the United States, although there is no legal definition for natural foods, there are numerous unofficial or informal definitions, none of which is applied uniformly to foods labeled "natural." Neither the Food and Drug Administration (FDA) nor the Department of Agriculture (USDA) has rules for "natural." The FDA explicitly discourages the food industry from using the term, but food manufacturers will often place a "natural" label on foods which contain heavily processed ingredients.

In the United Kingdom, the Food Standards Agency restricts the use of "natural" to foods that have "ingredients produced by nature, not the work of man or interfered with by man." The standard explicitly rules out "foods derived from novel processes, GM or cloning."

So yes, what I mean by the term is essentially what I meant in *Hungry for Health* when I discussed eating primitive and organic and omitting contaminated and adulterated foods. But there is an important aspect of eating natural that was not really covered before, one that need serious attention: Those "novel processes" like genetic modification.

Genetically modified food

 Genetically modified (GM) foods are foods derived from genetically modified organisms (GMOs) — that is, organisms that have had specific changes introduced into their DNA by genetic engineering (GE) techniques. Genetic engineering, in which the genes of one species are inserted into the DNA of an unrelated species, is the human manipulation of an organism's genetic material in a way that does not occur under natural conditions. The first organisms genetically engineered were bacteria in 1973 and then mice in 1974. Genetically modified foods were first put on the market in the early 1990s. The most common genetically modified foods are soybeans and corn.

Advantages of GM foods

Since commercial introduction of genetically modified food in 1996, the industry has ballooned, and more and more acres of land are now devoted to genetically modified crops. Cultivating GM crops has proved economically viable: Scientific evidence attests to GM crop's resilience to drought and diseases, the twin major sources of poor crop yields all over the world. And of course, better crop yields help to meet the nutritional needs of malnourished populations.

Multiple studies document gains in GM crops cultivation in the last decade. In *GM Crops: The Global Economic and Environmental Impact-The First Nine Years 1996-2004,* British economists Graham Brookes and Peter Barfoot note $27 billion in economic benefits, 172,000 tons less pesticide use by growers, and 14 per cent reduction in the environmental footprint associated with pesticide use.

Celebrants of GM crops laud their significant contribution to reducing greenhouse gas emissions by over 10 million tons (equivalent to removing five million cars from the road every year). As the world seeks solutions to destructive global warming-induced catastrophes, GM crops cultivation appears to provide one valuable solution. But before we all jump onto this fast-moving bandwagon that embraces GM technology, we should be asking, do the pros of GM crops outweigh their cons?

What's wrong with genetic engineering
-or- These genes don't fit

As we said, genetic engineering enables scientists to create plants, animals and micro-organisms by manipulating genes in a way that does not occur naturally. Apparently we *can* fool Mother Nature – but the joke may be on us!

Tampering with DNA is never a good idea, warns Dr. Joseph Mercola. The process of creating genetically modified organisms can cause all sorts of allergenic, toxic and carcinogenic side effects by producing proteins with new traits like herbicide tolerance or pesticide production. These GMOs can spread through nature and interbreed with natural organisms, thereby contaminating non-GE environments and future generations in an unforeseeable and uncontrollable way.

Pandora meets Frankenstein

This genetic pollution may constitute a major threat because GMOs cannot be recalled once released into the environment. In our zeal to avoid being swept away by the hurricane of hunger and the monsoon of malnourishment, we may be opening a veritable Pandora's Box of tiny plant Frankensteins that overtake the Earth one bean, seed or kernel at a time.

GM plants can "infect" non-GM plants and destroy their value. For example, GM papaya was first introduced in 1998. After six years, a test was conducted on 20,000 papaya seeds.

Although 80 percent were taken from organic farms, half of the seeds were found to be genetically modified! That means it is virtually impossible to safeguard non-GM crops from GM crops. And because the US does not require food companies to reveal the type of food used on their labels, people could be consuming GMOs without even knowing it!

Genetic roulette

In *Genetic Roulette: The Documented Health Risks of Genetically Engineered Foods,* author Jeffrey M. Smith declares that "Eating genetically modified food is gambling with every bite." (Smith is also the author of *Seeds of Deception,* the world's best-selling book on genetically engineered foods.)

In his new groundbreaking book outlining 65 health risks of foods that Americans eat every day, Smith shatters the biotech industry's claim that genetically modified foods are safe. Based on research studies and observational data and prepared in collaboration with a team of international scientists, the book also explains how safety assessments on GM crops are not competent to identify associated health problems.

Health risks of GM foods

GM crops are unusually hardy because of their

built-in pesticides. However, GM crops have abnormally high levels of toxins and suboptimal levels of nutrients. Genetic changes can alter thousands of natural chemicals in plants (phytonutrients), increase carcinogens, viruses, and other pathogens, and promote allergic responses.

Simply put, says Smith, "The two primary reasons why plants are engineered are to allow them to either drink poison or produce poison." Poison drinkers are called "herbicide tolerant" because they are outfitted with genes that allow them to survive otherwise deadly doses of toxic herbicides. The poison producers are the "Bt crops." Inserted genes from *Bacillus thuringiensis* (Bt), an insect-killing microorganism, produce a pesticide in every cell of the plant. Bt is thousands of times more concentrated and hence more toxic when built into crops than when used in its natural spray form.

When given a choice, pigs, chickens, buffalo, geese, elk, deer, raccoons, squirrels and rats all avoid GM foods. According to the American Academy of Environmental Medicine (AAEM), so should humans. "Several animal studies indicate serious health risks associated with GM food," including infertility, immune problems, accelerated aging, organ toxicities, and gastrointestinal disturbances. "There is more than a casual association between GM foods and adverse health effects," AAEM wrote. "There is causation...."

Of the major genetically modified food crops --

soy, corn, cottonseed, canola, summer squash, tomatoes, potatoes, and peas – all have demonstrated health concerns.

The "oy" in soy

GM soy accounts for about 90 percent of soybeans planted in the US; it is present in about 70 percent of all food products found in American supermarkets. GM soy (as well as corn and papaya) contain new proteins with allergenic properties. For example, soon after GM soy was introduced in the UK, soy allergies skyrocketed by 50 percent.

Allergies may be the least of our problems. Rats and mice fed GM soy showed lower birth weight, damaged sperm and reproductive ability, and increased mortality. According to PhysOrg.com, a Russian study found that 55.6 percent of the newborns of female rats fed GM soy before, during, and after pregnancy, died within three weeks. Only nine percent of the offspring of rats fed non-GM soy died. In addition, 36 percent of the rats in the GM-fed group were underweight, compared with only 6.7 percent of the control group. Mice fed GM soy had liver and pancreas problems and unexplained changes in testicular cells and sperm. GM soy also changed cellular metabolism in rabbit organs.

Corn porn

Rats fed GM corn approved for human consumption developed liver and kidney toxicity. In a study published in the *International Journal of Biological Sciences* analyzing the effects of

genetically modified foods on health in mammals, researchers found that agricultural giant Monsanto's GM corn was linked to organ damage in rats. Effects were mostly concentrated in kidney and liver function, but some effects on heart, adrenal, spleen and blood cells were also frequently noted. Mice fed GM corn had fewer and smaller babies. Pigs and cows became sterile from GM corn. In Germany and the Philippines, GM corn was blamed for the deaths of buffalos, cows, horses, and poultry.

Superweed cottonseed

Cottonseed plants, like genetically modified corn, soy, and canola, can crossbreed with wild species, creating "superweeds" requiring stronger and more environmentally hazardous herbicides that destroy beneficial species as well. Cotton plants that are modified to resist weevils are also not hospitable to monarch butterflies. In India, buffalo grazing on GM cottonseed displayed reproductive complications and infertility; thousands of grazing sheep died. Pigs in the US also became sterile or gave birth to bags of water. Sheep grazing on GM cotton developed enlarged bile ducts as well as severe irritation and black patches in their intestines, which ultimately caused their death.

Cottonseed oil from GM cotton plants, when consumed by humans and animals, may increase resistance to antibiotics. Dr. Mae Wan Ho, Director of the UK Institute for Science in Society, has called for destruction of GM cotton crops and a halt to production.

Can the canola

Three different mutant weeds resistant to three common herbicides – Monsanto's Roundup, Cyanamid's Pursuit, and Aventis' Liberty — were produced when Canadian farmers began planting GM canola seeds in 1995. Today 80 percent of the acres sown are genetically modified canola, and a 2010 study found transgenes in 80 percent of wild varieties in North Dakota. Because of excess toxic load, rats fed GM canola developed heavier livers than normal.

Squash the squash

According to research supported by the National Science Foundation, the prevalence of bacterial wilt disease is significantly greater on transgenic squash than on non-transgenic plants. Then when cucumber beetles feeding on infected plants deposit their bacteria-laden feces on the leaves, the bacteria find their way into the plant and ultimately to those who consume its produce. Genetic engineering also compromises the nutritional value of squash, as GM squash has been found to contain 68 times less beta carotene and four times more sodium than non-GM varieties.

Tomatoes, potatoes and peas

One third of rats fed GM tomatoes for 28 days got bleeding stomachs, and seven out of a group of 40 rats died within two weeks. Mice fed GM potatoes with inserted Bt pesticide showed intestinal damage. GM peas generated an allergic-type inflammatory response in mice.

Not so sweet sugar beet

Although health problems have not yet surfaced with GM sugar beets, legal problems have. Recently several groups led by the Center for Food Safety have sued the US Department of Agriculture for defying a court ban on GM sugar beet plantings. Over 95 percent of US sugar beet production is now grown from GM seeds altered to withstand Monsanto's Roundup herbicide. GM sugar beets are known contaminants of organic beets and Swiss chard.

Papaya, oh mya!

Similar issues are emerging with GM papaya in Hawaii, where independent laboratory tests revealed widespread contamination of papaya seeds sold by the University of Hawaii to places as far away as Thailand. Of the nearly 20,000 papaya seeds tested by Genetic ID laboratories — 80 percent of which came from organic farms — all showed a contamination level of 50 percent.

Live pesticide factories

Transfer of viral genes into gut micro-organisms may weaken both human viral and bacterial defenses in the mouth, throat and gut.

If Bt genes transfer to our digestive system, they could turn our gut bacteria into living pesticide factories. GM foods might also create antibiotic-resistant diseases, thus making gonorrhea and tuberculosis even harder to treat and proliferating more "superbugs" like *Methicillin-Resistant Staphylococcus Aureus* (MRSA). Disease-resistant crops may activate dormant viruses or promote new plant viruses, which carry risks for humans. Risks are greater for children, newborns and pregnant mothers.

GMO: Just say no!

We are just beginning to observe the genome-wide changes in gene expression created by artificial gene insertion. Genetic modification can disrupt DNA, create genetic instability and  mutations, produce unintentional RNA variations, switch on harmful genes, and lead to unpredictable health problems. Herbicide-tolerant crops increase herbicide and pesticide residues in food, which in turn can cause immune and endocrine disruption. In addition to bioaccumulation of toxins in the food chain, GM crops also increase environmental toxins.

Disturbing questions loom: Can't we find another way to solve the world's hunger problems without risking the health of those we would serve? Is it too late to turn the clock back? If organic seeds can no longer be trusted, how can we encourage people to eat organic? Or even a plant-based diet? The answers are unclear.

But a few things we do know for sure: (1) Abstaining from all food is not an option. (2) We don't need to add insult to injury: Eating as pure a diet as possible can only help. (3) There are still more toxins in animals than in plants. (4) Plants, especially those grown in mineral-rich soil, offer plentiful phytonutrients that can counteract toxins and protect our health in thousands of valuable ways. (5) Detoxification is more important than ever. In a famous laboratory experiment conducted by Dr. Alexis Carroll, chicken heart cells were potentially kept alive indefinitely. If the researcher failed to feed the cells for a few days, they still survived, but even one day without changing the water in their growing medium was enough to kill the cells. So keeping all of our eliminatory organs working efficiently can help us process out a load of poisons on a daily basis. (6) Organizations fighting for the purity of our food supply really deserve our support.

2. Eat Vegan

Many of my patients have declared they didn't know why they got sick because they had always "eaten healthy." As I often explain, (1) disease may not be so much about what you're eating as what's eating you, and (2) there are probably as many definitions of "healthy eating" as there are people trying to define it. So let's provide some clarity.

All kinds of consumarians

Vegan is not the same as vegetarian. There are fish-eating vegetarians, egg-eating vegetarians, and dairy-eating vegetarians. Some people may absolutely thrive on those types of diets, but not all vegetarians are healthy. Some vegetarians are really "starchetarians" in disguise. A Coke and a Danish qualify for "vegetarian" but certainly do not provide optimal nutrition. Neither do deep-fried batter-dipped vegetables nor frozen vegetarian dinners heated in a microwave oven. Foods that are micro-waved are not healthful, no matter how many plants they contain.

Of course, the best vegetarian diets are composed primarily of plants. Researchers at Loma Linda University School of Public Health studying 600,000 Seventh-day Adventists found longer than average life spans with lower rates of cancer and heart disease among those vegetarians raised on a heavily plant-based diet – the operative phrase here being a heavily plant-based diet.

Mothers not welcome

Donald Watson, founder of the very first Vegan Society, coined the term "vegan" in 1944 in order to differentiate vegetarians who ate dairy and egg products from those who did not. Veganism is an extreme type of vegetarian diet that excludes meat, fowl, fish, eggs, and dairy products. Said another way, vegans eat no food that had a mother!

Vegans also abstain from consuming any type of animal-derived ingredients such as whey, casein, gelatin, or other animal by-products. Many vegans do not eat any foods that have even been processed by the animal kingdom, including honey from bees. Although there is some debate as to whether such foods fit into a vegan diet, since this book is for vegans, we have chosen the side of conservatism and excluded honey as well.

Starchetarians and nutritarians

Back to our "starchetarians." A vegan diet should be more than just pasta, bread and potatoes (even if they are whole grain and organic). Just as organic food is about what's left in as well as what's left out, we wish to focus on veganism at its best – not just the exclusion of animal products, but also the inclusion of what is optimal — plentiful beans, legumes, vegetables, fruits, nuts, and seeds as well as whole grains, and the nearly infinite number of dishes made by combining them.

Joel Fuhrman, MD has coined a new word that describes this approach: *nutritarian.* Simply put, a nutritarian is a person whose food choices are influenced by nutritional quality, a person who strives for more micronutrients per calorie in his or her diet. Explains Fuhrman, "A nutritarian understands that food has powerful disease-protecting and therapeutic effects and seeks to consume a broad array of micronutrients via his/ her food choices. It is not sufficient to merely avoid fats, consume foods with a low glycemic index, lower the intake of animal products, [or eat a vegetarian diet]. A truly healthy diet must be micronutrient rich.... The foods with the highest micronutrient per calorie scores are colorful vegetables and fresh fruits. For optimal health and to combat disease, it is necessary to consume enough of these foods that deliver the highest concentration of nutrients."

No meat? What do you eat?

When you tell someone you're a vegan, you normally hear, "How do you get your protein?" The correct response will probably not go over very well: "The same as every other adult should be doing – eating very little."

Americans are obsessed with protein. Vegans are bombarded with questions about where they get their protein. Athletes think their performance depends on high protein. Protein supplements are sold at health food stores and juice bars. This concern about protein is misplaced. The average American eats 400% in excess of the recommended daily amount (RDA) for protein. Most of us don't need fish, fowl or animals to get our protein. Great plant protein sources are seeds, nuts, beans, legumes, whole grains and cereal grasses (especially quinoa, which contains all eight essential amino acids), sprouts, avocados and bananas. According to Brenda Cobb (*Healthkeepers Magazine*, October 2010), sprouted mung beans and lentils and juiced

No Meat??! What do you eat?

cereal grasses contain a higher percentage of protein than meat or chicken.

How much do we need?

Although protein is certainly an essential nutrient which plays many key roles in the way our bodies function, we do not need huge quantities of it. Wrote Harvey Diamond, "people who eat [a plant-based diet] over long periods of time or even lifetimes have no protein problems. The Hunzas,...Asians, and half a billion Hindus eat very little protein food...yet have no protein deficiencies."

In reality, we need only small amounts of daily protein, roughly only 10 percent — one calorie out of every ten we take in. For the average adult that amounts to only about 50 grams, or two ounces. So if you had a quarter pounder for dinner last night, you were double quota and we didn't even talk breakfast and lunch!

With protein, more than the RDA is not necessarily better. There do not appear to be any health advantages to consuming a high protein diet, and there appear to be distinct disadvantages. Excess protein can create a host of long-term health problems. We'll discuss this later.

Note: The Recommended Daily Amount (RDA) suggested for protein is between 0.8 and 1.0 grams of protein for every kilogram that we weigh (0.45 grams of protein per pound that we weigh). For the average adult that amounts to 150 lb divided by 2.2 kg = 68 kg = 54 to 68 g protein. Multiplying each gram of protein x 4 calories/gram = 216 to 272 calories from protein per day.

Where do you get your calcium?

The other question vegans get a lot is "What do you do for calcium?" What do the cows do? They produce calcium-rich milk but they don't consume milk as adults. They eat grass!

Green plants, more than dairy products, contain bio-available calcium along with magnesium and all of the other necessary co-factors for calcium utilization. Dairy industry marketers would have us believe otherwise, but milk is a mediocre source of calcium. Pound for pound, there is much more calcium in broccoli than in milk. And calcium without its co-factors is basically an osteoporosis waiting to happen! More on that later too.

Reasons to be vegans

Like the reasons to eat organic, the vegan diet is valuable for what it excludes as well as what it includes. That is, it avoids the negative effects of meat and embraces the positive effects of plants.

1. Disease prevention and longevity

The eating of animals can be hazardous to your health as well as theirs! The correlation between meat and dairy consumption and a wide range of degenerative diseases is well established. According to the American Dietetic Association, meat-eating has been linked with cancer, heart disease, strokes, diabetes, hypertension, osteoporosis, kidney stones, and many other disease conditions. The China Oxford Cornell Diet and Health Study, the world's largest study of diet and disease ever completed, found strong correlations between increased degenerative disease in China and the changeover from the traditional Asian plant-based diet to a western diet full of meat and dairy and fat. For more information on how specific diseases relate to diet, see Appendix A.

2. Increased energy and endurance

The idea that meat is needed for strength and energy is largely a fallacy. Scientific studies repeatedly show that a vegetarian diet based on whole grains, fruits and vegetables improves energy and endurance. Rich in complex carbohydrates and energy boosting vitamins and minerals, diets high in plants provide the optimal source for maximum and enduring strength.

The complex carbohydrates found in vegetarian foods are gradually digested, providing a steady source of glucose to the blood. Conversely, the fat and protein in meat are very difficult to digest. Eating meat can often take energy away from the rest of the body and cause people to feel tired and sluggish. Poorly digested flesh foods can stagnate in the bowels for up to three days and create a toxic overload that contributes to fatigue.

For most humans, a vegetarian diet can

improve stamina, concentration, and sense of well-being. In one study, athletes who switched to a vegetarian diet improved their endurance to almost three times as much as those who remained carnivorous. Another study, conducted by Yale professor Irving Fisher, compared the strength and stamina of active meat-eating athletes to that of vegetarian athletes and sedentary vegetarians. He found that flesh eaters had far less endurance than even sedentary vegetarians!

 The power of a balanced vegetarian diet is exemplified in the lives of many world class athletes. Ironman triathlete, two-time Canadian ultra marathon champion, and best-selling author on performance nutrition, Brendan Brazier is one of only a few professional athletes in the world whose diet is 100% plant-based. Similarly, Dave Scott, universally recognized as the greatest triathlete in the world, is also a vegetarian. He calls the idea that people, especially athletes, need animal protein a "ridiculous fallacy."

3. Reduction of toxins and contaminants

Flesh foods are loaded with dangerous poisons such as drugs, growth hormones, pesticides, and chemical preservatives. As these toxins are fat-soluble, they concentrate in the fatty flesh of the animals. So do viruses, bacteria, and parasites. Every year millions of people become sick after eating contaminated meat!

Though some may think eating "organic" meat is the solution, the fact is that dead animal flesh is inherently full of toxins and thus poisonous to the human system. Some of the most common and/or dangerous meat contaminants include livestock drugs, hormones, pesticides, chemical additives, pathogenic microorganisms, and parasites. For more of the gruesome details, see Appendix B.

Toxic Transit

Bowel function can be either our friend or foe. Fast transit time helps to detoxify poisons and avoid toxemia; slow transit time does the opposite. One reason that fiber intake is so important is that it speeds up intestinal transit time. Whereas plants are generally high in fiber content, meat, poultry and dairy products have none. Fiber can bind up and escort out circulating toxins, hormones, mutagens and carcinogens. Fiber absorbs excess fats, cleans the intestines, provides bulk, and aids in peristalsis. Meat, fish and eggs all move through the gastrointestinal (GI) tract slowly and decompose and putrefy extremely rapidly. Wholesome plant food travels quickly through the GI tract, leaving little time to spoil and incite disease within the body. Back to our reasons to be vegans.

4. Human anatomy

Many aspects of our bodies are by design vegetarian: our flat teeth are perfect for grinding grains and vegetables, not for tearing apart animal flesh. Similarly, our hands are designed for gathering, not for flesh-ripping. Our saliva contains the enzyme alpha-amylase, the sole purpose of which is to digest the complex carbohydrates in plant foods. (This enzyme is not found in the saliva of carnivores.) Basically we have all the right apparatus to consume vegetarian products, and none of the right apparatus for flesh foods. Our hands, teeth, feet, intestinal tract, and body chemistry are all more suited to being herbivores.

5. Moral and ethical reasons

Many world religions, including Buddhism, Hinduism, Seventh Day Adventism, and Mormon, all teach that eating animal flesh is wrong. Many great philosophers such as Plato, Socrates, Leo Tolstoy, and George Bernard Shaw have taught the morality of vegetarianism.

Love me, don't eat me.

When we consume animal flesh products other than for absolute survival, we are at odds with nature and lack compassion for at least some of our fellow living beings. Those who love animals find it abhorrent to kill them or cause them any harm. Animals which are raised for slaughter needlessly experience incredible suffering throughout their life and death. A committed vegan wrote on her blog, "Animals are God's property and have a right to life: the living beings temporarily encaged in animal bodies are not here for us to harm and exploit. We are meant to act as caretakers and protectors of animals and the planet, not exploiters and killers. I believe in nonviolence. Slaughter isn't."

6. Reduction of world hunger

By focusing on animals for food, we may be eating ourselves off the planet. Every day forty thousand children on this planet needlessly starve to death. According to the Department of Agriculture statistics, one acre of land can grow 20,000 pounds of potatoes, whereas that same acre of land, when used to grow cattle feed, can produce less than 165 pounds of edible cow flesh. In India, where cows are considered too sacred to eat, Dr. Ann Wigmore spent years working to reverse widespread starvation by teaching the value of green grasses and a plant-based diet. She established a number of healing camps, where she administered wheatgrass and live foods to hundreds of sick and malnourished men, women, and children. Wigmore published dozens of articles reporting the amazing rate of recovery experienced by many of these people.

7. Environmental protection

The raising of animals specifically to kill and eat them has resulted in incredible waste of our precious resources and devastation of our environment. A recent United Nations report concluded that a global shift toward a vegan diet is necessary to combat the worst effects of climate change. And the U.N. is not alone in its analysis. Researchers at the University of Chicago concluded that switching from a standard American diet to a vegan diet is more effective in the fight against climate change than switching from a standard American car to a hybrid. A German study conducted in 2008 concluded that a meat-based diet is responsible for more than seven times as much greenhouse-gas emissions as a vegan diet is.

Many leading environmental organizations, including the National Audubon Society, the Worldwatch Institute, the Sierra Club, the Union of Concerned Scientists, and Al Gore's Live Earth have recognized that raising animals for food damages the environment more than just about anything else that we do. The verdict is in: If you care about the environment, one of the single most effective things that you can do to save it is to adopt a vegan diet.

8. Financial costs

Consumers of plant based diets save money in terms of food costs and health care costs for themselves and the rest of society. Vegetarian foods tend to cost less than meat based items. Being healthier also means spending less on health care. Researchers have estimated that between $28.6 billion and $61.4 billion of the US health expenditures in 1992 could be attributed to meat consumption.

The bottom line

Given the devastating consequences of meat eating on an individual, social and ecological level, as thinking, caring beings we should choose plant-based diets. However, as I hope you will realize from the recipe section of this book, being a vegan doesn't mean you have to succumb to boring, bland, or uninspiring foods. A vegan diet can be vibrant and delicious. Instead of thinking about *what you can't eat,* think about *what you CAN eat,* and how eating that way helps your health, the economy, the planet, and the people and animals who live on it.

3. Eat Raw

*"To say that the body can easily digest
and assimilate cooked food properly
may someday prove to be the most grievous oversight
yet committed by science."*
– Ron Rendleman

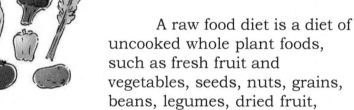

A raw food diet is a diet of uncooked whole plant foods, such as fresh fruit and vegetables, seeds, nuts, grains, beans, legumes, dried fruit, young coconut milk, seaweed, and of course pure water. Specific food preparation techniques that make raw foods more digestible and add variety to the diet include:

- Sprouting seeds, grains, and beans
- Juicing fruit and vegetables
- Soaking nuts and dried fruit
- Thermos-cooking grains
- Blending or processing any of above
- Dehydrating food (I did not include any such recipes because they require special dehydrating equipment)

Benefits of the raw food diet

Proponents of the raw food diet believe it confers numerous health benefits, including increased energy, improved skin appearance, better digestion and elimination, weight normalization, reduced risk of disease, and improved mental clarity. Several scientific articles contrast the benefits of a diet high in raw foods and the dangers of a diet high in cooked foods, especially when cooked at high temperatures.

Cooked foods, damaged goods

 Numerous research studies show that cooking often destroys vital nutrients. Depending on the cooking method, cooked food has much lower levels of vitamins and minerals than raw food. Most researchers agree that over 50% of B vitamins are destroyed by cooking, particularly thiamine (B1) and folic acid (losses up to 97%). Up to 80% of vitamin C is lost by cooking. The Max Planck Institute for Nutritional Research in Germany has found only 50% bioavailability in protein that had been cooked. Most importantly, cooked food lacks enzymes.

Essential e nzymes

There are three different categories of enzymes – metabolic enzymes, digestive enzymes, and food enzymes. Every organ and tissue in the body depends on its own specific set of metabolic enzymes which are responsible for repairing damage. Without these vital enzymes, organs and tissues – and ultimately the entire body – cannot survive.

Digestive enzymes are necessary to break down the foods we eat so their vital nutrients can be assimilated into the body. Whereas metabolic and digestive enzymes are made within our body, food enzymes come from the foods we eat. They start food digestion so the body does not need to produce so many digestive enzymes. However, unfortunately, food enzymes are highly susceptible to heat; they can be damaged or disenabled above 112 degrees F (100 degrees below boiling!) and often at temperatures as low as 96 degrees F. All cooked and processed foods are completely devoid of food enzymes, whereas the raw food diet is enzyme-rich. Intact food enzymes assist in digestion and absorption, while sparing enzymes for other important metabolic functions.

Dr. Edward Howell, a biochemist and nutrition researcher, documented over 50 years of research on the effects of enzymes on human health. In his book, *Enzyme Nutrition,* he notes that a lack of enzymes in the human body can lead to serious illness and even death. According to Dr. Howell, we have a fixed amount of enzymes that can be produced by the body in our lifetime, which he refers to as our "enzyme potential" or enzyme bank:

"It's just as if you inherited a certain amount

of money and didn't save any. If you spend it all, you won't have any more money in the bank. It is the same with enzymes. You inherit a certain enzyme potential and it must last a lifetime....the more you use your enzyme potential, the faster it is going to run out..."

On a raw food diet, the food enzymes begin the digestive process and therefore few digestive enzymes are needed, leaving ample metabolic enzymes for running the body. When we eat cooked food our bodies manufacture some of these digestive enzymes, but because cooked food is completely devoid of food enzymes that would have assisted in the digestion process, the pancreas and other digestive organs are forced to secrete large amounts of digestive enzymes, causing great stress on these organs and limiting the amount of metabolic enzymes that can be produced to heal, repair and run our organs. If they cannot be healed or repaired, numerous health problems could occur. On a cooked diet, it is common to see a weakened and or enlarged pancreas due to its being overworked. Day after day, year after year on a cooked diet will waste vital enzymes. When we are young, we have a large pool of enzyme potential to draw from, but as we age and our pool is depleted, eating cooked foods becomes more stressful on the body.

As Howell explains, when we eat cooked, enzyme-free foods we are stealing enzymes from our enzyme bank and thus from other parts of the body. This "stealing" of enzymes to service the digestive tract sets up a competition for enzymes among the various organ systems and tissues of the body. The resulting "metabolic dislocations" may be the direct cause of cancer, coronary heart disease, diabetes, and many other chronic incurable diseases. Howell formulated a basic enzyme axiom paraphrased thus: The length of life is directly proportional to the enzyme potential of an organism and inversely proportional to the rate of exhaustion of its enzyme potential.

Enzyme optimization

There are three ways to optimize enzyme function: (1) Even if you are eating cooked food, make sure you consume some raw foods at every meal. (2) Take food enzymes with cooked food. (3) Use simple food combining rules to allow foods to digest more completely. The most fundamental principle is to separate concentrated starches from concentrated proteins. So if you are consuming flesh foods, make certain that you do not have them with desserts, potatoes, or grains.

Electrical energy

Enzymes are catalysts for every biochemical reaction in the body. It is the enzymes in seeds that cause them to sprout; cook the seed and it will never, ever sprout. For that reason, cooking diminishes the "life force" of food, whereas raw food retains its life force. Centenarian Dr. Norman Walker stated emphatically: "The basic key to the efficacy of nourishing your body is the LIFE which is present in your food.... While it is true that cooked...foods sustain life, nevertheless that does not mean that they have the power to regenerate the atoms which furnish the life force to our body."

In *12 Steps to Raw Foods*, author Victoria Boutenko explains: "Inside plant cells, tiny organelles called 'mitochondria' break down carbohydrate and sugar molecules to provide energy. These organelles are alive and constantly at work, but only while the plant is alive, not after it is cooked. Consuming food that has life in it holds an immense benefit for humans. I have heard from many people that when they stopped eating cooked food, the very first change they noticed was a dramatic increase in their energy levels....."

Professor Hans Eppinger, chief physician at the First Medical Clinic of the University of Vienna, found that a live food diet specifically raises the electrical potential of the body's cells. "Live foods were the only type of food that could restore the micro-electrical potential of the tissues once cellular degeneration had begun to occur."

Dr. Gabriel Cousens, founding director of the Tree of Life Rejuvenation Center in Patagonia, Arizona, agrees that "by restoring the electrical potential of the cells, raw foods rejuvenate the life force and health of the organism. A live-food cuisine is a powerful, natural healing force which gradually restores the micro-electrical potential and overall functioning in every cell in our body."

Animals and raw food

In nature, observes Boutenko, wild animals eating entirely raw foods are free of the degenerative diseases that afflict humans. "Wild animals intuitively prefer fresher, more alive foods. If given a choice, goats, rabbits, and horses will always choose green grass over hay. We can find numerous examples in nature of various creatures that sustain themselves by eating live food only. For example, a caterpillar from Maui feeds solely on live snails. Most spiders consume exclusively live flies and bugs and would never eat dead insects....lizards would rather die from hunger than eat a dead bug...A cheetah eats only fresh meat...." Wild creatures that eat their natural raw foods diet rarely develop degenerative disease.

In contrast, it has become almost expected for domesticated animals to develop cancer, diabetes, arthritis, and other illnesses typical of humans.... A growing number of veterinarians contend that processed pet food is the main cause of illness and premature death in the modern dog and cat. According to the research of Dr. Gyorgi Kollath of the Karolinska Hospital in Stockholm, when young animals were fed cooked and processed food, they initially appeared to be healthy. However, as the animals reached adulthood, they began to age more quickly and developed chronic degenerative disease symptoms. Members of a control group of animals raised on raw foods aged less quickly and were free of degenerative disease.

Dr. Francis Pottenger was a physician well known for his studies on cats. In one of his studies, he fed half of his sick cats raw milk and raw meat, while the other half were fed pasteurized milk and cooked meat. The cats that were fed the cooked foods developed degenerative diseases, while those on raw foods remained disease-free for many generations. Upon autopsy, the cats on the raw diet had healthy pink organs and strong bones, whereas those on cooked foods had deteriorated organs and osteoporosis.

Linda Page, ND, in her book *Healthy Healing*, reveals that in cattle tests, calves given their own mother's milk that had first been pasteurized, did not live six weeks.

Neanderthals and Eskimos

 Scientific research indicates that much of human disease began when man started cooking his food. For example, 50,000 years ago, Neanderthals used fire extensively for cooking. From fossil evidence we know that the Neanderthal Man and his cave-dwelling companion, the cave bear, suffered from fully-developed chronic, deforming, crippling arthritis.

Is it possible that cold weather, not cooked food, was responsible for the arthritis of the Neanderthals? Not likely. The primitive Eskimo lived in an environment just as frigid as that of the Neanderthal Man. And yet, the Eskimo never suffered from arthritis and other chronic diseases. Why? Probably because he ate large amounts of raw food. The meat he ate was only slightly heated and was raw in the center. In fact, the word *Eskimo* itself comes from an Indian expression which means "he who eats it raw."

Most heart specialists would say that the diet of the primitive Greenland Eskimo, consisting of up to 10 pounds of meat and animal fats per day, was very dangerous. But the Greenland Eskimo did not suffer from high blood pressure, heart trouble or kidney stones.

Vilhjalmur Stefansson, an anthropologist who lived with and studied Eskimos, noticed that their diet consisted of 90% raw meat and fish. He concluded that they were free of modern-day diseases because they ate them raw. In fact, raw foods actually protect against heart disease. A study published in the *Journal of Nutrition* found that consumption of a raw food diet actually lowered plasma cholesterol and triglyceride concentrations.

Dr. Weston Price, a dentist from Cleveland, Ohio, was noted for his studies of vibrantly healthy indigenous cultures and their relationship to raw foods. On his travels around the world in the 1930s and 1940s, he found primitive cultures whose diets consisted of raw meats, eggs and dairy and who enjoyed superior health with no degenerative disease.

Cooking and cancer

Besides heart disease, arthritis, osteoporosis and aging, cooking also predisposes to cancer. According to an article published in *Cancer Epidemiology Biomarkers and Prevention* (Sept. 2004), "Possible mechanisms by which cooking affects the relationship between vegetables and cancer risk include changes in availability of... nutrients, destruction of digestive enzymes, and alteration of the structure and digestibility of some foods." Of 11 studies of raw and cooked vegetables, nine demonstrated a statistically significant inverse relationship of cancer with raw vegetables.

Dr. Norman Walker, DSc, PhD, a clinician, researcher, author, and specialist in raw foods, wrote: "People who live solely on fresh raw foods supplemented with a sufficient volume and variety of fresh raw vegetable and fruit juices, do not develop cancers."

The effectiveness of live foods and in particular fresh wheatgrass in preventing and reversing illness has been praised by Dr. Arthur Robinson, director of the Oregon Institute of Science and Medicine. In 1978 at the Linus Pauling Institute, Dr. Robinson completed a research project in which wheatgrass and live foods were fed to mice with squamous cell carcinoma. In Dr. Robinson's words, "The results were spectacular. Living foods alone decreased the incidence and severity of cancer lesions by about 75 percent. This result was better than that of any other nutritional program that was tried."

Max Gerson, MD, a German physician who documented case after case of patients who recovered from advanced and terminal cancer (*A Cancer Therapy: Results of 50 Cases,* 1958), successfully reversed disease by recommending a daily regimen of 12 glasses of fresh, raw vegetable juices.

Heated fats are damaged fats

Heating denatures fats, proteins and starches. Let's talk about fats first. Cooking destroys most of the nutritive value in fats, produces free radicals (lipid peroxides) in fats, and creates mutagenic and carcinogenic structures in fats. According to an article in *Environmental Health* (January 1981), "Heating of fats brings about measurable changes in their chemical and physical characteristics.... Thermally oxidized fats produced cellular damage in hearts, livers, and kidneys of lab animals." Heated fats and oils harden and produce plaques in the arteries, lymphatic system, and nerve endings.

Acrid acrylamide

Cooking also produces acrylamide, a chemical used in the manufacture of plastics. It was first discovered to be present in certain foods as the result of work announced in Sweden in 2002. Scientists at Stockholm University discovered that acrylamide is formed during the heating of starch-rich foods to high temperatures, while acrylamide levels are undetectable in uncooked foods. The higher the cooking temperature, the more acrylamide is formed.

Acrylamide is present in a disturbingly large number of foods, including potato chips, tortilla chips, taco shells, French fries, cakes, baked potatoes, biscuits, breads, cookies, crackers, and breakfast cereals (Swedish National Food Administration).

 According to Gabe Mirkin, MD, research in four countries suggests that French fries and potato chips may be a leading cause of cancer in the Western world. The World Health Organization (WHO) and the United Nations Food and Agriculture Organization (FAO) found that acrylamide levels in certain starch-based foods, particularly potato chips and French fries, were well above the level given in the World Health Organization's Guideline Values for Drinking Water Quality. Potato chips contain 500 times the maximum allowable amounts of acrylamide, and French fries sold in fast food chains contain more than 100 times the maximal allowable amounts.

The Swedish research and subsequent studies in Norway, Switzerland, the United Kingdom and the United States, have concluded that acrylamide causes cancer. In humans, acrylamide contributes to an increased risk of ovarian and endometrial cancers, renal cell cancers, and mouth cancers. In 2009 a Dutch study showed a positive association between dietary acrylamide intake and breast cancer. The highest consumption of acrylamide correlated with a 43% increase in breast cancer in women with estrogen or progesterone receptor positive cancers.

AGEs and aging

Acrylamide belongs to a class of particularly harmful substances in cooked food that form Advanced Glycation End Products (AGEs). AGEs are a group of molecules that are formed when heated sugars and starches attach to protein, particularly when cooked in the absence of water at very high temperatures and especially to the point of browning. (They do not form when food is cooked in water).

A study at Columbia University showed how cooking breads, crackers, cakes, cookies, and other grain products produce AGEs or glycotoxins. The National Research Council, in its publication *Diet, Nutrition and Cancer,* reported that cooked carbohydrates like fried potatoes or toasted bread produce mutagenic activity.

In the process of cooking, especially deep frying, glucose binds to proteins (in particular the amino acid *asparagine*) and forms abnormally tight (glycated) complexes. Explains Boutenko, "AGES have a pathological structure in which sugars and amino acids are strongly bound together in an irreversible connection.... There is a direct correlation between dietary AGE intake and a more rapid aging process."

Huge amounts of AGEs are formed at high temperatures. The Division of Experimental Diabetes and Aging in the Department of Geriatrics at the Mount Sinai School of Medicine in New York tested 250 foods for their AGE content. The amount of AGEs present in all food categories was related to cooking temperature, length of cooking, and lack of moisture. Broiling and frying resulted in the highest increased levels of AGEs, whereas the amount of AGEs in most fresh foods is relatively small. Among the highest sources of AGEs were foods like beef frankfurter, chicken breast, sautéed tofu, baked macaroni and cheese, French fries, thin crust pizza, and toasted cheese sandwiches, whereas the lowest AGEs were found in raw apples, bananas, fresh human milk, and fresh squeezed orange juice (*American Dietetic Association Journal*, April 2005).

AGEs can damage every tissue in the body. AGEs constitute a risk factor for cardiovascular disease, kidney damage, nerve degeneration and other chronic conditions. AGEs trigger inflammation, especially in patients with diabetes. By causing cross-linking reactions in the tissues of the body, AGEs progressively damage tissue elasticity and produce stiffening in blood vessels, the lens of the eye, the heart and other muscles. Age-related cardiovascular disorders that are linked to AGEs include arteriosclerosis, hypertension, stroke, and heart failure.

Diabetics form advanced glycation products in their bodies because high blood sugar levels cause sugar to stick on the protein in cell membranes, and it is these compounds that cause the horrible side effects of diabetes, such as blindness, deafness, heart attacks, strokes, kidney damage and nerve damage. HBA1C, the blood test doctors use to measure control of diabetes, actually measures the sugar bound to the protein on a person's cells. AGEs may also cause cancer, aging of tissues, arteriosclerosis, and high cholesterol, and are associated with loss of kidney function, Alzheimer's disease, thinning and wrinkling of skin and cataracts.

Heterocyclic amines

Another reason to eat raw and vegan: Cooking animal proteins such as steak and chicken at high temperatures and to the point of charring produces heterocyclic amines (HCAs). Known carcinogens, HCAs increase risk of cancer, especially colon cancer (*Cancer Epidemiology Biomarkers and Prevention*, June 2006). There is ample evidence that both HCAs and other compounds in cooked and processed meat and fish known as polycyclic aromatic hydrocarbons (PAHs) are mutagenic and carcinogenic (National Cancer Institute Nutrition Epidemiology Branch).

Nuke your microwave

Before we leave our discussion of raw foods, one crucial topic to address is microwave ovens. Any heat will destroy enzymes, but microwave ovens are  particularly destructive. To speak about the nutritional value of microwaved foods is to speak in oxymorons: there isn't any. At best, microwaving changes the chemical bonding and molecular structure of every food and beverage it touches, and at worst it actually creates immuno-suppressive and carcinogenic compounds.

One study published in *The Journal of the Science of Food and Agriculture* in 2003 found that broccoli "zapped" in a microwave lost up to 97% of its beneficial antioxidants. By comparison, steaming had only minimal effects, with only about 10% loss of antioxidant flavonoids.

Liquid Lies

As we will see, micro-waved milk isn't exactly milk -- how much more so baby formula, which is unsafe for babies, wrote Dr. Lita Lee of Hawaii in the Dec. 9, 1989 issue of *Lancet*: "Microwaving baby formulas converted... one of the amino acids, L-proline, ... to its d-isomer, which is known to be neurotoxic (poisonous to the nervous system) and nephrotoxic (poisonous to the kidneys). It's bad enough that many babies are not nursed, but now they are given fake milk (baby formula) made even more toxic via microwaving."

Micro-waved water isn't even water. Try these experiments: Goldfish placed in a bowl of cooled micro-waved water will die overnight. Plants watered with micro-waved water will wilt, wither, and dry up within a few weeks.

Don't try this experiment: In 1991, a hip surgery patient in an Oklahoma hospital died from a simple blood transfusion. It seems the nurse had warmed the blood in a microwave oven, a procedure which altered the blood enough to kill her.

What price convenience?

Over 90% of American homes use microwave ovens for meal preparation. Because microwave ovens are so convenient and energy efficient as compared with conventional ovens, very few homes or restaurants are without them. In general, people believe that whatever a microwave oven does to foods cooked in it doesn't have any negative effect on either the food or them. Of course, if microwave ovens were really harmful, our government would never allow them on the market, would they? Regardless of what has been "officially" released concerning microwave ovens, I have personally never used one based on the frightening research facts outlined below. Is it possible that millions of people are ignorantly sacrificing their health in exchange for the convenience of microwave ovens?

According to Anthony Wayne and Lawrence Newell in their article on "The Hidden Hazards of Microwave Cooking" (*Immune Perspectives* 2012), microwave cooking is not natural, nor healthy, and is far more dangerous to the human body than anyone could imagine. Of the hundreds of cancer patients we interview annually at the Center for Advancement in Cancer Education, an extremely high percentage have been heavy micro-wavers.

In *Health Effects of Microwave Radiation - Microwave Ovens,* Dr. Lee describes changes in the blood chemistries and in the rates of certain diseases among consumers of micro-waved foods. She notes that "Lymphatic disorders were observed, leading to decreased ability to prevent certain types of cancers. An increased rate of cancer cell formation was observed in the blood. Increased rates of stomach and intestinal cancers were observed. Higher rates of digestive disorders and a gradual breakdown of the systems of elimination were observed."

A disturbing study

Among the scientific research on micro-waved foods appears a famous short-term study which found significant and disturbing changes in the blood of individuals consuming micro-waved milk and vegetables. Eight volunteers consumed various combinations of the same foods cooked different ways. All foods that were processed through the microwave ovens caused changes in the blood of the volunteers. Hemoglobin and lymphocyte levels decreased, and overall white blood cell levels and cholesterol levels increased.

Dr. Hans Ulrich Hertel, a food scientist for many years with one of the major Swiss food companies, was the first scientist to conceive and carry out a quality clinical study on the effects of micro-waved nutrients on the blood and physiology of the human body. He and his associate, Dr. Bernard H. Blanc of the Swiss

Federal Institute of Technology and the University Institute for Biochemistry in Lausanne, published a research paper in 1991 indicating that food cooked in microwave ovens could pose a greater risk to health than food cooked by conventional means. The scientific conclusion showed that microwave cooking changed both the nutrients in the food and in the participants' blood, changes that could cause deterioration in the human system.

In intervals of two to five days, the volunteers in the study received one of the following food variants on an empty stomach: (1) raw milk, (2) the same milk conventionally cooked, (3) pasteurized milk, (4) raw milk cooked in a microwave oven, (5) raw vegetables from an organic farm, (6) the same vegetables cooked conventionally, (7) the same vegetables frozen and defrosted in a microwave oven, and (8) the same vegetables cooked in a microwave oven.

Blood samples were taken from every volunteer immediately before and at various intervals after eating the milk or vegetable preparations. Significant changes were discovered in the blood samples following the foods cooked in the microwave oven. These changes included a decrease in hemoglobin and the ratio of HDL (good cholesterol) to LDL (bad cholesterol). Lymphocytes (white blood cells) showed a more distinct short-term decrease following the intake of micro-waved food than after the intake of all the other variants.

According to Dr. Hertel, "Leukocytosis, which

cannot be accounted for by normal daily deviations, is taken very seriously by hematologists. Leukocytes are often signs of pathogenic effects on the living system, such as poisoning and cell damage. The increase of leukocytes with the micro-waved foods was more pronounced than with all the other variants."

Research on the health hazards of microwaving is not limited to the Swiss. Microwave ovens were invented by the Nazis to be used for troop support during the invasion of Russia. After the war, the Russians retrieved some microwave ovens and conducted thorough research on their biological effects. As a result, their use was outlawed in the Soviet Union and the Soviets issued an international warning on the health hazards, both biological and environmental, of microwave ovens. For more information on the disturbing findings of Russian researchers, see Appendix C.

Ten Reasons not to use your microwave

1.   Micro-waved diets cause digestive system disturbances.

2.   The human body cannot metabolize unknown by-products created in micro-waved food.

3.   The effects of micro-waved food by-products are permanent within the human body.

4.   Male and female hormone production is shut down and/or altered by continually eating micro-waved foods.

5.   Minerals, vitamins, and nutrients of all micro-waved food are reduced so that the human body gets little or no benefit, or the human body absorbs altered compounds that cannot be broken down for utilization.

6.   The nutrients in vegetables cooked in a microwave oven are altered into cancer-causing free radicals.

7.   Micro-waved foods cause stomach and intestinal cancers and may be a primary contributor to the rapidly increased rate of colon cancer in the U.S.

8.   The prolonged eating of micro-waved foods causes cancerous cells to increase in human blood.

9.   Continual ingestion of micro-waved food causes immune system deficiencies through lymph gland and blood serum alterations.

10.   Continually eating food processed in a microwave oven can produce virtually irreversible damage to the body's nervous system by "shorting out" electrical impulses in the brain and nerve centers. This can result in loss of memory, lack of concentration, emotional instability, and decreased intelligence.

In view of the extensive scientific research literature concerning the hazardous effects of direct microwave radiation on living systems, it is astonishing to realize how little effort has been taken to replace this detrimental cooking tool with technology more in accordance with nature. We recommend you throw out your microwave oven and use a toaster oven as a replacement. As an alternative, turbo or convection ovens are rapid, safe options; they cost just about the same as microwave ovens, and with circulating hot air they heat food in 50% less time than most conventional ovens. In summary, microwave ovens make excellent boat anchors. If you don't have a boat, just unplug your oven and store your healthy cookbooks in it. Starting with this one.

How much raw food?

So out with microwaves, HCAs, acrylamides and AGES. In with enzymes. Lots of them. But does our diet have to be 100% raw? How much raw food is necessary and how do we optimize its intake? At minimum, consume a diet that contains at least 50% raw foods by volume daily, and aim for a diet that is 75% living or raw. More than half the recipes in this book and its predecessor book, *Hungry for Health,* are uncooked.

You can't really overeat on raw foods. First, they are usually so nutritionally dense that small amounts are really satisfying. Second, they are generally much lower in calories than animal products, so you can consume a lot of volume without gaining weight.

Mark Rosenberg, MD, of the Institute for Healthy Aging, tells his patients to aim for 7-12 servings of fresh fruits and vegetables per day to get optimal levels of antioxidants, vitamins, minerals and phytonutrients. New guidelines from the US Department of Agriculture are actually 13 servings! The easiest way to do that? Combine several servings of fruit and vegetables together, either blended or juiced.

Benefits of Juicing

- Freshly juiced produce contains **concentrated enzymes** that are essential to digestion, metabolism, and conversion of the food you eat into the nutrition your body needs.

- Fresh juicing contains **concentrated phytochemicals** and antioxidants — nature's "doctors" — that boost your immune system, neutralize free radicals, regulate hormone levels, and fight disease.

- Juicing supplies **concentrated amounts of vitamins and minerals**, like the B vitamins, Vitamin C, magnesium, potassium, etc., that preserve skin and muscle integrity and boost mental well being.

- Juicing can be custom-tailored to **target certain health issues**, like weight loss, heart health, and detoxification, by combining produce containing specific nutrients.

- Juicing allows you to **absorb larger quantities** because the fiber has been removed and the digestion period is much faster than trying to digest the solid food. (One pound of produce yields about 12 ounces of juice. Imagine eating an entire bag of carrots versus drinking a glass of juice!)

Juicers vs blenders

Both blended and juiced veggies are extremely valuable. However, there is a difference between juicing and blending. "Total juicers" are really high-powered blenders that include all the fiber of the plant. Juicing is done in a juice extractor, designed to remove the fiber. So now I hear you asking,"I thought fiber was good for you!" It is, but as we just mentioned, separating juice from fiber allows much higher quantities to be absorbed much more efficiently. On the other hand, because juiced fruit minus fiber is going to cause blood sugar spikes, fruits should mostly be blended, which keeps the fiber with the juice.

When juicing vegetables, use about 80% dark green vegetables like kale, spinach, broccoli, and parsley, as these vegetables are not only packed with antioxidants and phytochemicals and loaded with chlorophyll for blood building and healing; they are also very low in sugar. Then add a small amount of carrot, beet or apple to sweeten.

The best time to drink your juices is on an empty stomach, between meals, or at least 30 minutes before a solid food meal, to allow your body to absorb the nutrients from your juice. Consuming juices with a meal is better than not consuming them at all, but the work you just did to spare digestive energy by separating the juice from the fiber is undone if you consume the juice with solid food. (That may be necessary for people with hyperglycemia). If you

are not going to juice on a regular basis, at least take Juice Plus+, an extremely well researched encapsulated nutraceutical product made from the extracted juices of 17 different chemical-free plants.

4. Eat Native

"Polar bears in the Sahara Desert
are apt to find themselves in serious trouble."

—David Katz, MD, MPH
Director, Prevention Research Center
Yale University School of Medicine

In his introduction to *The Way to Eat*, Dr. David Katz declares that the Sahara is not where polar bears belong. "Not being in the environment for which all of their remarkable adaptations prepare them places the polar bears in jeopardy.... Polar bears are designed to retain and conserve heat.... In the Arctic it keeps them alive. In the Sahara it would threaten their survival."

"Just like polar bears," continues Katz, "human beings, *homo sapiens*, are a species. And, like all species, we have a native habitat and a relationship with it. We have compensated admirably for climate and terrain, using our ingenuity to devise air conditioning and heating systems, building materials, and clothes for heat and cold. But we are [also] adapted to a particular *nutritional* environment, and in moving outside of it, we have not done so well.... We are confronted with a modern nutritional environment that is at odds with our every trait and...that is in many ways toxic to us, very much like polar bears in the Sahara."

So while we discuss the health consequences of a diet heavy in animal fats and protein, we must also consider the environment in which they are eaten. The traditional diet of native Indians from the far north Canadian Rocky Mountains, for example, consisted almost entirely of wild animals, principally moose and caribou. Dr. Weston Price, on visiting this area in the 1930s, explained that winter temperatures of 70 degrees below zero made it impossible to grow cereal grains or fruit; yet Price found no tooth decay or degenerative disease in this population.

In marked contrast, on his visits to Polynesia, Fiji and Tahiti, Price found that severe health challenges had developed among the previously robust South Sea Islanders who abandoned their native diet of mostly raw shellfish and fish.

Among the Amazon Jungle Indians, those who

consumed a native diet of tropical vegetables, fruits, and fish enjoyed perfect dentition and perfect health; not so those of the same race who abandoned their native diet and adopted the diet of missionaries.

Whale of a tale

Among the northern Inuit of Greenland, whale blubber formed an important part of the traditional diet (Smith 2009), yet atherosclerosis was more or less unknown. The average 70-year-old Inuit with a traditional diet of whale and seal had arteries as elastic as that of a 20-year-old Dane (Mulvad and Pedersen, 1992). In the 1970s there was not a single death due to cardiovascular disease among the 3000 inhabitants of the Uummannaq district of Greenland. However, those who emigrated to Denmark contracted the same diseases as the rest of the population (*Atherosclerosis*, 2004). A subsequent rise in cholesterol and triglycerides among the Inuit was closely associated with the westernization of their diet.

In studies of people living in Vilcabamba Valley in the Andes Mountains of southern Ecuador, researchers found an extraordinarily high percentage of vigorous, active adults living well past 100 years, all with no signs of cancer, heart disease or diabetes – diseases that were common in towns just 50 miles away. When the centenarians moved down the mountain to be near younger relatives, their health changed with their diets.

In his landmark book *Nutrition and Physical Degeneration*, author Weston Price (the "Charles Darwin" of Nutrition) offers a thorough and fascinating discussion of what happens when modern food is introduced to native populations. Price also makes a case for the idea that saturated fat and cholesterol alone may not be the evils that they have been said to be and that manmade processed food is really the problem, along with not eating right for your particular body type, genotype, genetic code, metabolic type or constitution.

Monkey business

The Awaji Island Monkey Center in Hyogo, Japan, is a sad illustration of the dangers of abandoning a native diet. Prior to its establishment in 1967, the percentage of deformed births among the area's monkey population was about one percent. But since human feedings began there and the monkeys abandoned their traditional diet of leaves, fruit, nuts and insects, the percentage of deformity has accelerated dramatically.

Deformed monkeys have been born in the group every year since 1969. By 1983, 63 out of 271 monkeys had been born deformed, and out of 37 groups that have adapted to being fed by humans, 20 had deformities. External deformities mainly appeared in the monkeys' hands, feet and limbs, particularly split, twisted, joined, lacking or short fingers and toes. The monkeys also produced successively weaker generations – external deformities followed by internal deformities followed by miscarriages followed by still births followed by sterility.

Minoru Nakahashi has devoted the last 32 years of his life to the monkeys of Awajima, working hard to increase public awareness of the deformities at the center. Mr. Nakahashi insists that the problem of deformity among the Japanese macaque monkeys is essentially embedded in our modern, industrial society, which has resulted in abandonment of traditional diets, unleashing of toxic, man-made pesticides, and environmental destruction, in the drive to maximize production, consumption and economic growth. A full understanding of the deformed monkey issue involves seriously addressing, reevaluating and transforming the assumptions, perceptions and values of modern industrial society.

The paleo diet

One of the core principles in *Hungry for Health* is to Eat Primitive. Until 10,000 years ago, humans were hunter-gatherers, and no known society farmed animals or grew crops. The modern dietary regimen known as the "Paleolithic diet" (also popularly referred to as the "caveman diet" or the "hunter-gatherer diet") is based on the ancient ancestral diet of wild plants and animals that the human species habitually consumed during the Paleolithic Era—a period of about 2.5 million years that ended around

10,000 years ago with the development of agriculture.

First popularized in the mid 1970s by a gastroenterologist named Walter Voegtlin, and discussed by Drs. Boyd Eaton and Melvin Connor in the *New England Journal of Medicine* in 1985, the concept of Paleolithic Nutrition is based on the premise that modern humans are genetically adapted to the diet of their ancestors. Loren Cordain, PhD, a foremost authority on the evolutionary basis of diet and disease, coined the term "Paleo Diet" in his book of the same name (2002).

All of these scientists maintain that the ideal diet for human health and well-being is one that closely resembles the ancestral diet of lean meat, fish, vegetables, fruit and nuts, while excluding grains, legumes, dairy products, salt, refined sugar, and processed oils. Paleolithic hunter-gatherers were naturally thin and largely free of conditions like cancer, heart disease, diabetes, osteoporosis, arthritis, gastrointestinal disease, autoimmune disease, and acne. By eating the foods that we are genetically adapted to eat, followers of the Paleo Diet enjoy similar health.

Greens not grains

Eating "native" also means eating few grains. Because grain was not part of man's original diet but was a later addition when he changed from a hunter-gatherer lifestyle to one of cultivation, many people have allergies or sensitivities to grains, especially to the gluten-laden grains. (Sprouted grains are much better tolerated because sprouting activates enzymes needed to digest them.)

According to Dr. Joseph Mercola, for over five hundred generations, humans existed primarily on a diet of wild animals and vegetation. It was only with the advent of agriculture a mere 10,000 years ago – an extraordinarily small period in evolutionary time – that humans began ingesting large amount of grains. Since nearly all of our genes were set before the advent of agriculture, in biological terms, our bodies are still those of hunter-gatherers, not grain eaters.

After the advent of agriculture, societies that transitioned from a primarily meat and vegetation diet to one high in grains generally show reduced life spans, increases in infant mortality and infectious diseases, and higher nutritional deficiencies. Keep in mind that these ancient societies used entirely unrefined and organic grains. Today over 90% of grains are highly processed, making the negative consequences of grains far worse.

Because of the physiology of contemporary humans has not changed much from that of our distant ancestors, our bodies have never adapted to the excessive amount of carbohydrates from grains (and sweets) in our present-day diet. In fact, since our diet is still largely based on what Mercola calls the "severely misguided" 1992 USDA Food Pyramid — which recommends an "atrocious" 6-11 servings of breads, cereals, rice and pasta per day — this surplus of insulin-spiking carbohydrates is the main reason for our epidemic of obesity and diabetes.

They call it gluten for a reason

White flour has only one role and you learned about it in kindergarten: paper mache. You take the flour and the water and you make a paste –  so if you want to glue up your intestines, this is a really good way. Scientists have learned that the proteins in grains – especially wheat protein — gluten – are very difficult to digest. Besides wheat, gluten is also found in spelt, barley, rye, and some oats.

A diet high in cooked grains puts an enormous strain on the digestive system. (This is one reason traditional cultures invariably soak or sprout grains before eating them.) Asians tolerate grains better than other populations probably because of the length of time their societies have lived on grains; their pancreas and salivary glands (starches break down primarily by the salivary amylase enzyme) are up to 50% heavier in proportion to body weight than are those of Westerners.

Grain intolerance, especially inability to process gluten, can result in allergies, celiac disease, inflammatory bowel syndrome, chronic indigestion, gut enteropathies, eliminatory problems, candida albicans overgrowth, immune compromise and/or autoimmune disease. Non-gluten grains are often better tolerated. Rice, quinoa, and millet are more easily digested than wheat.

Eat Seasonal

Another aspect of eating "native" is eating local and in season. Eating in accordance with what's in season in your particular region has many advantages, including nutritional value and environmental value. "The closer we eat to the source, and the less processing and shipping, the

more nutritional value we can access. And there is less fuel used, and less waste in the environment," says Terry Walters, author of the seasonal cookbook *Clean Food* (2009).

As Walters points out, imported produce usually travels thousands of miles to reach your local grocery store. Have you eaten a tomato recently? Chances are it was grown halfway around the world, picked green, shipped thousands of miles, and then ripened with ethylene gas. Imported tomatoes travel an average of 1,569 miles, whereas one grown in your region in season may have traveled just 60 miles.

In fact, thanks to advances in transportation, growing methods, and booming global commerce, today's food shopper can buy raspberries from Chile or asparagus from Australia when they're nowhere near in season locally. But just because we can, should we?

There are numerous health benefits associated with seasonal eating. The body naturally needs different foods during specific times of the year—foods that protect us from the effects of seasonal changes—say experts such as Elson M. Haas, MD, author of *Staying Healthy with the Seasons* (2004). Haas' recommendation draws on nutritional wisdom from Traditional Chinese Medicine (TCM). For example, in TCM, spring is associated with the liver—one of the body's primary detoxification organs. Spring is also the time when dandelion and other greens are fresh and available. "Young, bitter-tasting greens support the liver's function and its ability to cleanse the blood," says Rebecca Wood, author of *The New Whole Foods Encyclopedia* (Penguin, 2010).

In a research study conducted in 1997 by the Ministry of Agriculture, Fisheries and Food in London, England, significant differences were found in the nutrient content of milk in summer versus winter. Iodine was higher in the winter; beta-carotene was higher in the summer. The Ministry discovered that these differences in milk composition were primarily due to differences in the diets of the cows. Similarly, researchers in Japan found three-fold differences in the vitamin C content of spinach harvested in summer versus winter.

Cooking methods also play an important role in seasonal eating. We naturally crave hot soups in fall and early winter. Eating cold, uncooked foods during fall and winter can put stress on the body; it further chills you and takes extra energy to digest, putting a drag on your system. However, in the summer, we eat more raw foods—so our homes and our bodies don't get overheated when it's already hot. Every season has a specific health focus, with seasonal foods and cooking methods that support the body during that time.

There was a time when the human race had no choice but to eat what nature provided. Food was about fuel, and fuel was about hunting, foraging, gathering, and eating what was available. Today's food shopper has choices our ancestors never dreamed of. Any time of the year, you can go to the grocery store and buy produce that was once available for only a few months or weeks of the year. You can have strawberries in November, tomatoes in December, and corn on the cob in February! Given these options, why would one want to eat like our ancestors did, eating produce in season? Because it's better for you.

Seasonal eating is in vogue, but it's hardly a new trend. Eating foods when nature produces them is what people the world over have done naturally through most of history, before supermarkets dotted the landscape and processed foods became ubiquitous. Seasonal eating is also a cornerstone of several ancient medical traditions, which view it as integral to good health.

Seasonal eating means two things, really: building meals around foods that have just been harvested at their peak and adjusting your diet to meet the particular health challenges of winter, spring, summer and fall. While it may seem like a luxury to have any food we want, anytime we want it, eating foods in season offers many benefits.

Eat Local

> *"Shipping is a terrible thing to do to vegetables. They probably get jet-lagged, just like people."*
> —Elizabeth Berry

Eating seasonally often means eating locally grown foods. "Eat local" has become one of the mantras of the new environmental movement. Why is this important? Consumption of locally produced food supports small and midsize local farmers, and cuts down on pollution from shipping and trucking food.

Locally grown food also often means more nutritious food. Fruits and vegetables that will be traveling long distances to market aren't picked when they are ripe – when produce is at its peak nutritional value — but rather before ripeness. While the produce might gain color and softness on its journey to the supermarket, nutritional value comes through the stem from the living plant. Once harvested, a vegetable is as nutritious as its going to get. And in a double whammy, nutritional value actually decreases every day past harvest. Produce picked and eaten at its peak generally has more vitamins, minerals and antioxidants than foods harvested before they're ripe and then shipped long distances. For example, one Penn State study found that spinach lost most of its folate and carotenoid concentrations after eight days of storage.

So local means freshest. If we all ate right out of our own organic gardens, that would be ideal. The next best scenario is to purchase produce within 24 hours of being picked from local farm stands or from small neighborhood food coops, without going through giant distribution centers (which can add hours and days to deliveries). Sounds good, right?

Closer is not always safer

Unfortunately, eating local has its problems. While consumers may think locally grown food is safer, food safety experts say that's not necessarily true. Many "locally grown" products are not organic or even pesticide-free. And while freshness is more likely if food isn't trucked so far, food-safety experts say there's no evidence that locally grown products are safer, especially because small producers often lack the food-safety audits more common among big producers, such as audits that check for evidence of insects on produce like leafy greens and fresh fruit. Undetected outbreaks of food-borne illnesses are more likely with local products delivered in small quantities and sold in a small area.

Eating local also has it semantic problems. Like the term "natural," there are no regulations specifying what "local" means. Retailers have far broader definitions of "local" than consumers do. Wal-Mart, the nation's biggest retailer, considers a food local if it's grown in the same state as it's sold, even if that's a state as big as Texas and the food comes from a farm half the size of Manhattan. Whole Foods, the biggest retailer of natural and organic foods, considers local to be anything produced within seven hours of one of its stores. For Seattle's PCC Natural Markets, foods are termed local if they come from anywhere in Washington, Oregon or southern British Columbia.

So do your local best without driving yourself crazy. If you allow yourself to get drawn into an all-or-nothing mindset, the proposition will seem impossible. You will get caught up in "local" semantics or derailed by the list of the imported foods you think you can't live without. Bananas. Coffee. Chocolate. Eating locally is about doing what you can. It is about making the most of your region's agricultural strengths. It is about focusing on whole foods, because highly processed foods are made with many ingredients that are shipped from afar, processed, and shipped again.

Simpler is better

Bottom line, what we are really talking about is eating simply. Simpler is better. Eat real foods, mostly if not all of them plants, and whenever possible consume them unprocessed, uncooked and untrucked.

Remember, too, as I reminded my readers in *Hungry for Health*, you don't need to do a perfect job. Our Creator gave us only one mouth and six eliminatory organs – so we only have to get it half right. Health is not about perfection, it's about balance. Even as you climb your ladder of nutritional sophistication. Even if you're a vegan. Even my most seriously ill clients. You have to cheat on my diet; it's absolutely required! Because if life isn't worth living, why bother fighting to be well? So no guilt! Guilt is more carcinogenic than any dietary indiscretion, so eat what you feel good about, and feel good about what you eat. Eating or moving to a plant-based diet is easier than you think. Enjoy!

RECIPES

APPETIZERS & SNACKS

Antipasto

¼ C extra virgin olive oil
3 T balsamic vinegar
½ t dried basil
½ t dried oregano
¼ t sea salt
Pinch pepper
6 leaves romaine lettuce
1 C whole button mushrooms
7 oz jar roasted red peppers, drained and sliced
14 oz can non-marinated artichoke hearts, drained
1 C whole black olives

Arrange the lettuce leaves on a large serving platter and set aside. In a small mixing bowl, whisk together oil, vinegar, herbs, salt and pepper. Add mushrooms to marinade, coat well, and place in one corner of serving platter. Continue with other vegetables. Pour remaining marinade over platter and serve.

Yield: 6 servings

*"In general, mankind,
since the improvement in cookery,
eats twice as much as nature requires."*

Benjamin Franklin

Avocado Stuffed Celery

1 stalk celery
1 ripe avocado
1 t finely chopped onion
¼ t lemon juice
Pinch cayenne pepper
Pinch paprika

Wash, dry and cut celery stalk into 2 inch pieces. In a small mixing bowl, mash avocado. Add lemon juice, onion, and cayenne and mix well. Stuff into celery pieces and sprinkle paprika on top.

Yield: 10-12 hors d'oeuvre

TASTY TIP:
For a colorful variation, omit paprika and spread onto grape tomato halves.

"One of the basic laws of life is to eat our foods whole, organic, and in their natural, raw state."

Gabriel Cousens, MD

Banana Oat Bran Muffins

1½ C oat bran
½ t baking powder
¼ t sea salt
2 T Sucanat (dried cane juice)
1 T lemon juice
1 small apple, peeled and grated
3 speckled bananas
¼ C chopped walnuts
2 T raisins
3/8 C water

Preheat oven to 375 degrees. Stir together oat bran, baking powder, salt and Sucanat in a large bowl. Set aside. In another bowl, mash bananas. Add lemon juice, apple, walnuts, raisins and water. Combine wet and dry ingredients well. Spoon into sprayed muffin tins but do not overfill. Bake for 30 minutes. Remove from tins and place on cooling rack.

Yield: 12 muffins

HELPFUL HINT:
You can use ½ C unsweetened applesauce in place of raw grated apple.

"Every human being is the author of his own health or disease."

Buddha

Black Bean and Avocado Canapes

½ C canned black beans, rinsed and drained
1 firm ripe Hass avocado, diced
1 scallion, finely chopped
1 t extra virgin olive oil
Dash salt
Pinch pepper
20 artichoke bottoms or large scoopable corn
    chips

In a medium bowl, combine the beans, avocado,
scallions, oil, salt and pepper. Gently press 1 T
bean mix onto each artichoke bottom or chip.

Yield: 20 canapes

NUTRI-NOTE:
Black beans get their dark color from anthocyanins, powerful antioxidants with potential health effects against cancer, aging, diabetes, and neurological diseases.

*"I don't understand why asking people to eat
a well-balanced vegetarian diet is considered drastic,
while it is medically conservative to cut people open
and put them on cholesterol-lowering drugs
for the rest of their lives."*

Dean Ornish, MD

Blueberry Quinoa Muffins

1 C quinoa flakes
½ C chopped walnuts or pecans
2 t aluminum-free baking powder
1 t baking soda
1 T Sucanat
½ t sea salt
2 speckled ripe bananas
2 T maple syrup
2 t salba (chia seeds), ground
½ C water
½ C blueberries

Preheat oven to 400 degrees. In a medium sized bowl, mix together quinoa, nuts, and other dry ingredients and set aside. In a small mixing bowl, mash bananas. Stir in syrup, salba and water. Mix well. Add to bowl of dry ingredients and incorporate thoroughly. Gently fold in blueberries. Spoon into sprayed muffin tins filled about ¾ to the top. Bake for 18 minutes.

Yield: 12 muffins

HELPFUL HINT: Serve with your favorite unsweetened fruit spread.

*"Those who think they have no time
for healthy eating
will sooner or later have to find time for illness."*

Edward Stanley

Collard Wraps

5 leaves fresh collard greens
1 ½ C shredded carrots
½ C raw pine nuts
¼ C raisins
2 T extra virgin olive oil
1 t dried or 2 t chopped fresh mint leaves
1 T lemon juice
½ small onion, finely chopped
1 clove garlic, minced

Rinse collard greens and pat dry. Remove stems and spine. Cut large leaves down the middle. Set aside. Place all remaining ingredients in a large bowl and combine well. Spoon carrot mixture in the center of a collard leaf. Fold over the outer edge, fold in one end of the leaf, and roll. Fasten with a toothpick and place on serving plate. Repeat with remaining leaves.

Yield: About 16 wraps

NUTRI-NOTE:
Collard greens are an excellent source of vitamins B6 and C, carotenes, chlorophyll, and fiber. They are also a good source of minerals like iron, copper, and calcium and manganese.

"He that takes medicine and neglects diet, wastes the skill of the physician."

Chinese Proverb

Maple Walnut Bread

2 very ripe bananas
1 ¼ C almond meal flour
¾ C walnuts, coarsely chopped
½ C water
¼ C pure maple syrup
¼ C oat bran
¼ C unsweetened applesauce
2 T arrowroot
2 T salba, ground
1 ½ T raw almond butter
1 T Sucanat
2 t baking soda
1 t walnut oil
1 t vanilla extract
½ t ground cinnamon

Preheat oven to 350 degrees. Grease a 4 by 9
loaf pan with walnut oil. In a large mixing bowl, sift
together almond meal, oat bran, arrowroot,
Sucanat, baking soda and cinnamon. Stir in
chopped walnuts and set aside. In a medium
bowl, mix together salba and water. Add bananas
and mash with a fork. Stir in remaining wet
ingredients. Add contents of medium bowl to dry
ingredients and incorporate thoroughly. Pour
into loaf pan. Bake 60 minutes or until cake tester
or bamboo skewer inserted into center of loaf
comes out clean. Allow bread to cool completely
before turning out onto plate. With a sharp knife,
cut into slices about ¾ inch thick. Store
remaining bread in refrigerator.

Yield: 1 loaf

Masala Lentil Spread

2 C water
1 C dry lentils, rinsed
1 T curry powder
4 t Sucanat
½ t sea salt
½ t turmeric
¼ t ground coriander

Place lentils and water in a pot, bring to a boil, then simmer, covered, about 40 minutes or until all the water has been absorbed. Mash lentils and set aside. Combine spices and seasonings in a small bowl. Add to lentils and mix well. Serve warm or cold with chips.

Yield: 2 C

NUTRI-NOTE:
Lentils support heart health and help fight cancer. The compound curcumin found in curry and its main ingredient turmeric can protect against breast, prostate, lung and colon cancer.

"The foods we eat either create health or disease."

T. Colin Campbell, PhD

Oven Kettle Popcorn

6 C air popped popcorn
¼ C brown rice syrup
1 ½ t walnut oil
1 t apple cider vinegar
½ t sea salt

Preheat oven to 325 degrees. Put popped corn
into a large bowl. Thoroughly mix all of the other
ingredients in a small bowl. Pour over popcorn
and stir until popcorn is completely coated. Bake
12-15 minutes, checking often to prevent burning.
Remove from oven and serve warm.

Yield: 6 cups

NUTRI-NOTE:
Brown rice syrup is
considered to be
one of the healthi-
est of natural
sweeteners
because its low
glycemic index will
not elevate blood
sugar.

*"Most medical problems and medical tragedies
we face in the modern world
are the result of nutritional folly."*

Joel Fuhrman, MD

Refried Bean Dip

3 cans (15 oz) red kidney beans, rinsed and
    drained
1 small onion, finely chopped
2 T red wine vinegar
1 t sea salt
1 t ground cumin
1 t dried oregano
1 t freeze-dried garlic
¼ t chili pepper sauce
1 t Liquid Smoke

Place all ingredients in food processor and blend
until very smooth. Transfer to a serving bowl,
cover and refrigerate. Serve with rice crackers,
organic corn chips, or celery chunks.

Yield: 4 C

NUTRI-NOTE:
This dish offers
nearly 50g of
protein and 50g
of fiber to divide
among your
guests!

*"The smarter we get the sicker we become,
because we are looking for cures instead of causes."*

Joel Robbins, MD

Rice Crust Pizza

2 8-inch rice tortillas
¾ C marinara sauce
12 baby spinach leaves
1 C Daiya vegan mozzarella style shreds

Turn oven on broil setting. Spray cookie sheet
with all natural olive oil spray. Place tortillas on
sheet, place under broiler and toast lightly about
30 seconds on each side. Remove from oven.
Spread sauce over each tortilla to within ½ inch
of edges. Place 6 spinach leaves on each tortilla
and sprinkle mozzarella cheese atop the spinach.
Place under broiler about 90 seconds until
cheese melts. Remove from oven. Slice each
tortilla into quarters and serve.

Yield: 8 slices

HELPFUL HINT:
Do not overcook;
remember those
acrylamides!

*"Eating much larger amount of the right foods…is the
secret to long-term weight loss and great health."*

Joel Fuhrman, MD

Roasted Mushrooms with Garlic

8 medium white mushrooms
4 very large garlic cloves, thinly sliced
4 t extra virgin olive oil
Pinch sea salt
1 t dried rosemary, finely ground

Preheat oven to 350 degrees. Grease large flat baking pan with 1 t olive oil. Wash mushrooms and remove stems. In a small bowl, whisk together garlic, salt and rosemary with the remaining olive oil. Spoon into mushroom caps. Place mushrooms on pan and bake for 25 minutes.

Yield: 8 hors d'oeuvre

NUTRI-NOTE: Garlic has a strengthening, laxative effect, relieves indigestion, disinfects the stomach, and kills bacteria in the large intestine.

"Nothing will benefit human health and increase the chances for survival of life on Earth as much as the evolution to a vegetarian diet."

Albert Einstein

Roasted Red Pepper Hummus

1 can (19 oz) chickpeas, rinsed and drained
7 oz jar roasted red peppers, drained and
  chopped
3 T lemon juice
1 clove garlic, minced
½ t sea salt
½ t extra virgin olive oil
½ t ground cumin
Pinch cayenne pepper

Place all ingredients except roasted peppers in a food processor and blend until very smooth. Add peppers and blend briefly. Transfer to a serving bowl, cover, and refrigerate for at least one hour before serving.

Yield: 1 ¼ C

TASTY TIP:
Serve as a dip for chips or cut raw vegetables, stuff into celery chunks or mushroom caps, or spread on rice crackers.

"To eat is a necessity,
but to eat intelligently is an art."

La Rochefoucauld

Stuffed Baby Bella Mushrooms

8 oz baby bella mushrooms
¼ C raw almonds
¼ C walnuts
1/4 medium onion, chopped
1 stalk celery, chopped
1 small carrot, chopped
2 inch cauliflower floret
1 small clove garlic, minced
1 t raw agave nectar
Dash sea salt

Wash mushrooms and remove the stems, setting them aside for stuffing. Place almonds and walnuts in food processor and process until finely ground. Place remaining ingredients in food processor and mix thoroughly. Stuff into mushroom caps and serve.

Yield: 10 hors d'oeuvre

TASTY TIP:
For additional flavor, marinate mushrooms overnight in a mixture of ¼ C extra virgin olive oil and 2 T balsamic vinaigrette before stuffing.

"The more high-nutrient food you consume, the less low-nutrient food you desire."

Joel Fuhrman, MD

Sweet Potato Canapes

1 medium sweet potato or yam, scrubbed
½ zucchini
½ medium onion, diced
1 ½ t raw almond butter
1 ½ t pure maple syrup
20 pecan halves
Dash salt
Pinch pepper

Preheat oven to 400 degrees. Bake potato 45 minutes or until soft. Steam fry onion with 1T water in small frying pan over medium heat for 10 minutes, adding water by the tablespoon as needed. Place onion, potato, almond butter, maple syrup, salt and pepper in food processor and process until smooth, scraping sides of bowl periodically. Slice zucchini into 1/8 inch slices and spread sweet potato mixture by the teaspoon onto each slice. Garnish with a pecan half.

Yield: about 20 canapes

TASTY TREAT: Cucumbers, celery slices, or rice crackers may be substituted for zucchini.

"Those who think they have no time for healthy eating will sooner or later have to find time for illness."

Edward Stanley

Tacos with Guacamole and Beans

1 ripe avocado
2 t lemon juice
1 clove garlic, minced
2 t extra virgin olive oil
1 C kidney beans, rinsed and drained well
7 oz jar roasted red peppers, drained and thinly
    sliced
1 C shredded romaine lettuce
2 T minced red onion
Dash sea salt
Pinch black pepper
5 6-inch 100% corn tortillas

In a food processor, combine avocado, lemon juice, garlic, 1 t olive oil and 1 pinch salt until well blended. Set aside. In a medium bowl, combine beans, onion, black pepper, and remaining oil and salt. Heat a skillet over medium heat and lightly heat each tortilla prior to assembly. To assemble, spread taco with guacamole, then top with small amount of red pepper strips, lettuce and bean mixture in that order. Roll taco and fasten with a toothpick.

Yield: 5 tacos

*"Phytochemicals hold a special, elite place
in the nutritional landscape."*

Joel Fuhrman, MD

Thai Spring Rolls

¾ C So Delicious coconut milk
½ C 100% peanut butter
1 T wheat-free tamari
1T arrowroot powder
2 t Sucanat
2 t chili sauce
8 spring roll rice wrappers
½ C chopped romaine lettuce
½ C shredded carrots
½ C mung bean sprouts, rinsed
¼ C shredded unsweetened coconut

In a blender, combine coconut milk, peanut butter, tamari, arrowroot, Sucanat and chili sauce until smooth. Place romaine, carrots, sprouts, and coconut into separate small bowls and set aside. Spread wet tea towel on a flat surface. Dip one wrapper into hot water for 15-20 seconds. Remove with tongs and gently lay flat on towel. Spoon 1 T of peanut sauce, 1 T of coconut, and 1 T of each of the vegetables into center of wrapper. Fold bottom up just enough to cover the filling, fold in the sides tightly, and roll wrapper upwards to form a tight roll. Repeat with all 8 wrappers. Use remaining peanut sauce for dipping.

Yield: 8 spring rolls

*"Just as food causes chronic disease,
it can be the most powerful cure."*

Hippocrates

Walnut Garlic Pate

1 ½ C raw walnuts
1 clove garlic, diced
¼ small onion, chopped
1 stalk celery, chopped
3 T fresh parsley
1 T balsamic vinegar
1 T extra virgin olive oil
¼ t sea salt
Dash stevia powder

Process garlic, onion, celery and parsley in the food processor until very finely chopped. Add walnuts, vinegar, oil, salt and stevia and blend until smooth. Serve on rice crackers or packed into celery slices.

Yield: 1 ¼ C

NUTRI-NOTE:
Walnuts are one of the best plant sources of protein. They are rich in fiber, B vitamins, magnesium, and vitamin E, and have high amounts of immune-boosting omega 3 fatty acids.

"To prevent and reverse...most of the chronic disease in the modern world, you don't need instructions from a doctor's prescription pad.
The prescription is nutrition."

Joel Fuhrman, MD

White Bean Dip with Cucumber Spears

15 oz can cannellini beans, rinsed and drained
2 medium cloves garlic, diced
1 t extra virgin olive oil
1 T lemon juice
¼ t salt
Dash pepper
1 large cucumber, peeled
Dash paprika

Place all ingredients except cucumber into food processor and blend thoroughly until creamy. Transfer to a small bowl and place in center of round serving platter. Top with a sprinkle of paprika. Slice cucumber in thirds crosswise, then in eighths lengthwise. Arrange cucumber spears, spoke-like, around perimeter of platter.

Yield: 3 servings

"Cooking or other forms of processing destroy qualities and components of our food for which the significance is not yet, or perhaps never will be, known in its totality."

Gabriel Cousens, MD

Yogurt with Blueberries

1 container (6 oz) So Delicious vanilla-flavored
   coconut milk yogurt
2 T golden flaxseeds
¼ C blueberries
2 T hulled hempseeds

Place yogurt into small mixing bowl. In a coffee
mill, grind flaxseeds about 10 seconds to a fine
meal. Stir into yogurt. Divide yogurt in 2 small
snack bowls. Place 2 T blueberries atop each
portion of yogurt. Sprinkle with 1 T hempseeds
each.

Yield: 2 filling servings

"The best six doctors anywhere
And no one can deny it
Are sunshine, water, rest, and air
Exercise and diet.
These six will gladly you attend
If only you are willing
Your mind they'll ease
Your will they'll mend
And charge you not a shilling."

Nursery Rhyme

Zucchini Garbanzo Tacos

4 6-inch 100% corn tortillas
2 T extra virgin olive oil
2 T Daiya mozzarella-style shreds
1 green onion (scallion), diced
1 medium zucchini, diced
¼ medium onion, diced
¼ red bell pepper, diced
¼ C cooked garbanzo beans (chickpeas)
1 clove garlic, minced
1 t cumin
1 t lemon juice
¼ t sea salt

In a bowl, combine zucchini, bell pepper, garlic, cumin, salt, and 1 T olive oil. Stir to coat and allow to sit for about 10 minutes. In another bowl, toss together garbanzo beans, scallion, and lemon juice and set aside. Heat remaining olive oil in a large fry pan, and sauté onions over medium heat for about 5 minutes until translucent. Add to chickpea mixture. Transfer zucchini mixture to fry pan and sauté for about 10 minutes. Add garbanzo mixture, stir, and remove from heat. Warm tortillas slightly in oven or steamer basket. In the center of each tortilla, place about 1 heaping teaspoon of "cheese" shreds and top with garbanzo/zucchini mixture. Roll tortillas, fasten with a toothpick and serve.

Yield: 4 tacos

SOUPS & BROTHS

Asparagus Soup

1 lb asparagus
1 T extra virgin olive oil
1 small onion, chopped
2 ribs celery, chopped
16 oz vegetable cooking stock
1 ½ C water
1 t dried oregano
½ t thyme
Salt and pepper to taste (optional)

Cut off hard stalk ends of asparagus and discard. Cut asparagus crosswise in 1 inch pieces. Heat oil in pot and cook asparagus, onion and celery until soft, about 5 minutes, stirring frequently. Add broth and water and bring to a boil. Add herbs, reduce heat to simmer, and cover. Cook 15 minutes.

Yield: 4-5 servings

NUTRI-NOTE:
Asparagus is an alkaline food with an abundance of an amino acid called asparagine that helps to cleanse the body of waste material.

*"When diet is wrong, medicine is of no use.
When diet is correct, medicine is of no need."*

Ayurvedic Proverb

Bean Soup with Kale

3 T extra virgin olive oil
1 C chopped onion
½ C chopped carrots
½ C chopped celery
½ t sea salt
2 garlic cloves, minced
4 C vegetable broth
1 bunch kale, stemmed and chopped
1 can (15 oz) cannellini beans, rinsed and drained
1 can black beans, rinsed and drained
½ t pepper
1 T red wine vinegar
½ t dried rosemary

Heat oil in large pot. Add onion, carrot, and celery and sauté 6 minutes or until tender. Stir in salt and garlic and cook one minute more. Stir in broth and kale. Bring to a boil. Add cannellini, black beans, and pepper. Cover, reduce heat, and simmer 15 minutes. Stir in vinegar and rosemary.

Yield: 6 servings

"Eat food, not too much, mostly plants."

Michael Pollan

Black-Eyed Pea and Sweet Potato Soup

1 large onion, finely chopped
3 cloves garlic, minced
6 C vegetable broth
¼ C tomato paste
2 cans (15 oz each) black-eyed peas, rinsed and
    drained
1 t Liquid Smoke
2 t dried oregano
1 bay leaf
½ t sea salt
¼ t cayenne pepper
1 lb sweet potatoes, peeled and diced
3 C thinly sliced and tightly packed collard greens

In a large soup pot, steam-fry the onion and garlic for 5 minutes over medium heat. Cook about 5 minutes, stirring frequently, and adding water by the tablespoon (1 or 2) as needed to prevent sticking. Place all other ingredients in pot. Cook, covered, over medium low heat for 40 minutes. Remove the bay leaf and serve.

Yield: 6 servings

*"You can repair cellular damage
simply by using nature..."*

Gary Null, PhD

Butternut Squash Soup

10 oz. butternut squash chunks
1 medium onion, peeled and coarsely chopped
1 apple, peeled and cored
2 C vegetable stock
1 oz. vanilla-flavored coconut or almond milk
1 T extra virgin olive oil
½ T curry powder
½ T maple syrup
1 T tapioca starch
½ t dried parsley or 1 t fresh diced parsley
Dash cinnamon
Dash sea salt
Pinch pepper

Cut squash and apples into 1- inch chunks. Puree in food processor and set aside. In a large soup pot, sauté the onions in oil over medium heat for 3 minutes. Add squash, apples, stock, curry, syrup, tapioca, cinnamon, salt and pepper. Bring to a boil, then simmer covered for 25 minutes. Stir in coconut or almond milk and simmer 2 minutes more. Transfer to serving bowls and garnish with a pinch of parsley.

Yield: 3-4 servings

Carrot Cashew Soup

1 ¾ C vegetable broth
14 oz. So Delicious vanilla flavored coconut milk
3 large carrots, sliced into pennies
1 medium onion, diced
¼ C raw cashew nuts
1 T tapioca starch
1 ½ t curry powder
Dash ginger powder

In a large cooking pot, combine broth, carrots, onion, curry and ginger and simmer over medium low heat for 20 minutes. Pulverize cashews in food processor. Add carrot broth, cashews, and tapioca to a blender jar and liquefy. Return to soup pot, stir in coconut milk, and serve.

Yield: 4 servings

HELPFUL HINT:
One can of sulfite-free coconut milk may be substituted for the refrigerated coconut milk.

"Nature itself is the best physician."

Hippocrates

Chilled Plum Soup

2 lbs (about 8) ripe plums, pitted and quartered
2 C fresh orange juice
1 C almond flour
¼ C sliced or slivered almonds
3 T Sucanat or dried cane juice
1 T fresh lemon juice
 1 t ground cinnamon
½ t orange zest

In a large soup pot, combine plums, orange juice, Sucanat, lemon juice, cinnamon and orange zest. Cover and cook medium-low for 15 minutes. In 2 batches, transfer to a blender, adding ½ C almond flour to each batch. Blend at low speed until well mixed. Transfer batches back to soup pot and refrigerate for at least 2 hours. Stir before pouring into serving bowls. Sprinkle with almonds and serve.

Yield: 6 servings

NUTRI-NOTE:
Plums are an excellent source of Vitamins A and C, calcium, magnesium, iron, potassium, and fiber.

"Not man made drugs but organic minerals and nutrients from God's good earth are needed by every cell, nerve, organ and tissue of your body."

Robert H. Sorge, N.D., Ph.D

Cold Peach Soup

4 ripe peaches, brushed well
1 t lemon juice
2 t almond extract
1 ½ C vanilla-flavored almond milk
4 T tapioca flour
½ t dried basil
6 small fresh basil leaves

Slice open peaches, remove stones and cut into chunks. Place all ingredients except fresh basil into a blender and puree well. Chill. Place basil leaves atop soup and serve.

Yield: 3 servings

NUTRI-NOTE:
Peaches must be organic; sprayed peaches contain higher levels of pesticides than any other fruit.

"Out of all the species…
man alone tries to cook and change his food."

Satya Sai Baba

Creamy Carrot Cauliflower Soup

1 head cauliflower, cut into florets
6 medium carrots, peeled and cut into ½ inch
   slices
5 C water
2 large cloves garlic, peeled and halved
1 stalk celery, diced
1 medium onion, cut into chunks
1 t sea salt
2 t dried parsley
½ t turmeric
¼ t pepper
1 t cinnamon
2 t maple syrup

Pour water into large soup pot. Add carrots and cauliflower and bring to a boil. Lower heat to medium, cover, and cook 10 minutes. Add celery, onion and garlic and cook, covered, another 6 minutes. Pour half of the vegetable and water mixture into a blender and puree. Transfer pureed soup to another soup pot. Pour the remaining half into the blender, add seasonings and maple syrup, and puree. Transfer to second pot and mix well. Pour into serving bowls and serve immediately.

Yield: 6 servings

TASTY TIP:
Add seasonings at the end of cooking; extended boiling can cook the flavors out.

Green Soup

1 fuji apple, washed and cored
4 stalks celery
1 ripe avocado
1 ½ C water
1 C stemmed parsley
3 T fresh bean or lentil sprouts, rinsed well

Chop apple and celery into one inch chunks.
Place into food processor with avocado and
parsley. Process together, slowly adding water,
and puree until creamy. Refrigerate for about 1
hour. Pour into serving bowls and garnish with
sprouts.

Yield: 3 ½ C

NUTRI-NOTE:
Celery is rich in
potassium and
sodium. Eating
this soup after a
workout is great
for electrolyte
replacement.

*"The news isn't that fruits and vegetables
are good for you. It's that they are so good for you
they could save your life."*

David Bjerklie

Mineral Broth

½ bunch of celery
5 medium carrots, scrubbed well
1 leek
1 small onion
3 large cloves garlic, diced
½ lb sweet potato (about 1 large)
2 sundried kombu strips, 7 inches each
1 ½ C kale, stripped from stems and chopped
12 C water

Chop celery, carrots, leek , onion, and sweet potato into ¼ to ½ inch pieces. Place into deep soup pot. Add garlic, kombu strips, kale and water. Bring to a boil, then reduce heat and simmer, covered, 1 hour. Using a slotted spoon, remove vegetables and reserve for stuffing or mulching. Serve clear broth.

Yield: 10 C

NUTRI-NOTE: Kombu is a Japanese sea vegetable very high in iodine and other important minerals like potassium, magnesium, and sodium.

"Consuming phytochemicals is not optional."

Joel Fuhrman, MD

Mulligatawny Soup

1 T cold pressed extra virgin olive oil
1 medium onion, chopped
4 cloves garlic, minced
1 T curry powder
2 t ground coriander
1 t ginger (fresh grated or powdered)
1 t ground cumin
1 t ground turmeric
¼ t ground cinnamon
¼ t ground cloves
¼ t black pepper
4 C vegetable broth
1 C water
1 C lentils, rinsed and drained
1 apple, peeled, cored and chopped
1 carrot, peeled and sliced into pennies
1 large potato, peeled and cubed
1 can (13.5 oz) coconut milk
1 T chopped fresh cilantro
1 t tamarind concentrate

In a small bowl, measure out dry spices and seasonings and mix well. Set aside. Place oil in a large soup pot and heat over medium setting. Add onions and stir fry for one minute. Add garlic and stir fry for two minutes more. Stir in spice mixture for about 20 seconds. Add broth, lentils, potatoes, carrots and apple. Cook, covered, over medium-low heat for about 25 minutes. Using an immersion blender, process until mostly pureed. Mix tamarind paste with a few drops of warm water until smooth. Add tamarind, coconut milk and cilantro leaves to soup and stir until heated through.

Yield: 6-8 servings

Onion Soup

1 ½ Vidalia onions, finely chopped
¼ C extra virgin olive oil
 C Madeira or red cooking wine
16 oz vegetable broth
½ t sea salt
Dash pepper
½ C Daiya vegan mozzarella style shreds

Preheat oven to 400 degrees. In a large soup pot, sauté onions in oil for 8 minutes over medium-high heat, stirring frequently. Remove from heat. Place half the onions into blender with broth, wine, salt, and pepper and liquefy. Return to pot and cook over medium heat for about 15 minutes, stirring occasionally. Transfer soup to oven-safe soup tureen or casserole or to individual baking ramekins. Spread mozzarella shreds over top and bake an additional 10 minutes or until cheese melts.

Yield: 4 servings

NUTRI-NOTE: Some studies have shown that increased consumption of onions reduces the risk of head and neck cancers.

*"Leave your drugs in the chemist's pot
if you can heal the patient with food."*

Hippocrates

Parsnip Soup with Broccoli

2 ½ C water
2 large parsnips, washed and scraped
3/4 C broccoli florets, diced
Pinch sea salt

Cut parsnips into ½ inch diameter chunks. In a medium pot, bring water to boil. Add parsnips and simmer, covered, for 15 minutes. Pour into blender and blend on lowest speed until well pureed. Return to pot, add broccoli and sea salt, and simmer 15 minutes until broccoli is soft.

Yield: 3 servings

NUTRI-NOTE:
Parsnips are low in calories, high in complex carbohydrates and insoluble fiber, and a source of vitamin C and folate.

"Supplements can't match or duplicate all the protective, strengthening elements of real fruits and vegetables."

Joel Fuhrman, MD

Red Lentil and Sweet Potato Soup

5 C vegetable broth
2 C cubed peeled sweet potatoes (about 1
   medium potato)
2 small onions, finely chopped
2/3 C red lentils, rinsed
½ t cumin
¼ t salt
Pinch white pepper

In a large soup pot, steam-fry the onions over
medium heat until soft, adding water by the
teaspoon to prevent sticking. Add broth,
potatoes, lentil, cumin , salt and pepper, and stir
well.   Bring to a boil, then simmer, covered, for
about 45 minutes or until lentils are tender. Serve
hot.

Yield: 6 servings

NUTRI-NOTE:
Lentils are an
excellent source
of protein and
fiber. 2-4 servings
per week can cut
breast cancer risk
by 25%.

*"Eat breakfast like a king, lunch like a prince,
and dinner like a pauper."*

Adele Davis

Shitake Mushroom Bisque

1 large Vidalia onion, chopped
¼ C extra virgin olive oil
16 oz vegetable broth
½ C Madeira or red cooking wine
4 oz white or baby bella mushrooms, chopped
4 oz shitake mushrooms
¼ t sea salt
Dash black pepper

In a soup pot, saute onion in olive oil over medium heat for about 6 minutes or until soft, stirring occasionally. Add white mushrooms and sauté 3 minutes more, continuing to stir. Remove from heat and place in blender. Add broth, wine, salt and pepper and blend until smooth. Return to soup pot. Remove stems from shitakes and discard. Slice mushrooms in very thin strips and add to blended mixture. Cook at medium-low temperature for about 20 minutes, stirring often.

Yield: 3-4 servings

TASTY TIP:
For a richer, creamier bisque, substitute 8 oz coconut milk for half of the vegetable broth.

*"The more we worry about nutrition,
the less healthy we seem to become."*

Michael Pollan

Sweet Cocoberry Soup

12 oz. So Delicious vanilla flavored coconut milk
   yogurt
1 C strawberries (leaves removed) or raspberries
¼ C unsweetened apple juice
½ t almond extract
2 fresh mint leaves

Puree all ingredients together. Pour into serving bowls and chill. Garnish with mint and serve.

Yield: 2 servings

HELPFUL HINT:
For pre-chilled soup, use ice crusher function of blender on frozen strawberries, blend with other ingredients, and serve.

*"Your health is dependent
on the nutrient-per-calorie density of your diet."*

Joel Fuhrman, MD

Tomato Rice Soup

3 C fresh tomatoes, skins removed
1 ½ T tomato paste
¾ C chopped onion
1 clove garlic, minced
1 stalk celery, chopped
1 carrot, chopped
1 t dried basil
1 t dried parsley
2 t brown rice syrup
1 C cooked brown rice
2 ½ C water

Combine all ingredients in a sauce pan except rice and rice syrup. Bring to a rapid boil. Reduce heat and simmer for approximately 40 minutes. Remove from heat and pour into blender. Add rice syrup. Blend until smooth. Pour soup back into sauce pan and add rice. Simmer about 10 minutes.

Yield: 4 servings

NUTRI-NOTE: Cooking tomatoes releases the lycopene, a carotene protective against prostate, breast, and lung cancer.

"He that takes medicine and neglects diet wastes the skills of the physician."

Chinese Proverb

Vegetable Bean Soup

2 ribs celery, chopped
1 medium carrot, peeled and sliced into pennies
1 medium onion, finely chopped
1 red pepper, chopped
2 cloves garlic, inced
3 T water
4 C vegetable broth
2 cans (15 oz) black beans
1 can (15 oz) canned diced tomatoes
1 C frozen corn
1 t cumin
1 t dired oregano
1 t dried basil
¼ t pepper
¼ t sea salt

In a large soup pot, sauté celery, carrot, onion, and garlic in 3 T water over medium high heat, stirring frequently, about 8 minutes or until onion becomes translucent. Add vegetable broth, beans, and tomatoes. Bring to a boil, then reduce heat to low. Add spices and seasonings and simmer, covered, for 15-20 minutes. Add corn and cook another 5 minutes.

Yield: 10 servings

NUTRI-NOTE:
One cup of cooked beans per day can help lower cholestorol, reduce cancer risk, and improve bowel function.

SALADS & DRESSINGS

Arugula Strawberry Salad

4 C baby arugula, rinsed, dried and packed tightly
6 large strawberries, stemmed, rinsed, and dried
½ C sliced almonds

Place 1 C greens on each salad plate. Slice berries top to bottom and arrange slices around perimeter. Sprinkle almonds atop greens. Serve with raspberry vinaigrette dressing.

Yield: 4 servings

NUTRI-NOTE:
Arugula is a dark leafy green in the cruciferous family of vegetables. It is closely related to broccoli, cauliflower, and brussel sprouts, some of the most potent anti-cancer foods around.

*"When diet is wrong medicine is of no use.
When diet is correct medicine is of no need."*

Ancient Ayurvedic Proverb

Beet Salad Vinaigrette

1 large red beet, shredded
4 T extra virgin olive oil
¼ t sea salt
 Dash black pepper
1 T apple cider vinegar
1 t finely chopped scallion
½ t maple syrup
¼ t Dijon mustard
3 C mixed baby greens
1/2 C coarsely chopped walnuts

Combine vinegar, scallions, syrup, mustard, salt and pepper in a blender and mix well.   While blender is still running, slowly add oil until emulsified. Toss beets with 1 t dressing and set aside. Toss greens with remaining dressing. Place mound of beets in center of greens and arrange walnuts around greens.

Yield: 3 servings

NUTRI-NOTE:
There is no better cleanser for your liver than fresh beets.

*"An ordinary pig knows more about diet
than the most learned college professor."*

J. Harvey Kellogg, MD

Berry, Radicchio and Mango Salad

2 C butter, bibb or Boston lettuce, shredded
2 C shredded radicchio
1 C strawberry slices
1 small ripe mango, peeled and diced
1 ½ C fresh raspberries
¼ C water
2 T apple cider vinegar
2 T extra virgin olive oil
2 T maple syrup
Dash salt
Pinch pepper
4 T walnut halves

Place lettuce and radicchio shreds into mixing bowl. Add strawberry and mango and toss well. Divide among individual salad plates. Place raspberries in a blender with the water, cider vinegar, olive oil, salt and pepper and puree until smooth. Spoon dressing over each plate. Top each plate with 1 T walnuts.

Yield: 4 servings

TASTY TIP:
Shredded red cabbage may be substituted for radicchio, and blueberries may be substituted for strawberries.

Black Bean and Corn Salad

15 oz can black beans, rinsed and drained
10 oz package frozen corn, thoroughly defrosted
1 small onion, minced
1 small red pepper, diced
2 scallions cut into thin rings
1 T Liquid Smoke or natural hickory flavoring
2 T extra virgin olive oil
2 T apple cider vinegar
2 t Dijon mustard
1 t ground cumin
Salt and pepper to taste

Combine beans, corn, onion, red pepper, and scallions. Set aside. Place oil, vinegar, mustard, cumin, Liquid Smoke, salt and pepper in blender and process for 15 seconds. Pour dressing over vegetable mixture, toss well and serve.

Yield: 5-6 servings.

NUTRI-NOTE:
Beans help to control insulin and blood sugar levels.

*"When the nutritional landscape of America
is shaped by nutrient density…
we will have dramatically extended
our healthy life expectancy."*

Joel Fuhrman, MD

Caesar Salad

8 C shredded romaine lettuce
½ C water
2 T lemon juice
1 T extra virgin olive oil
1 T wheat-free tamari
½ t maple syrup
2 T Dijon mustard
6 T raw pine nuts
Pinch pepper
2 large cloves garlic, minced
5 T Daiya mozzarella style shreds
Fresh milled pepper (optional)

Place lettuce shreds in a large mixing bowl. Set aside. Pour water, lemon juice, oil, tamari and syrup into blender. Add mustard, garlic, pine nuts and dash pepper and blend at medium speed until creamy. Pour over romaine and toss well. Place onto individual serving plates. Sprinkle mozzarella shreds over top of each salad. Top with fresh ground pepper if desired.

Yield: 5 servings

"People could extend their lifespans by 20 or more years – just by maintaining proper enzyme levels."

Dr. Edward Howell

Carrot Pineapple Salad

2 C finely grated carrots
½ C diced fresh pineapple
¼ C raisins
1 T extra virgin olive oil
1 T lemon juice

Combine all ingredients thoroughly in a medium bowl.

Yield: 2-3 servings

NUTRI-NOTE:
This salad, eaten daily for a week, helps to cleanse the liver.

*"More die in the United States
of too much food than of too little."*

John Kenneth Galbraith

Carrot Pistachio Salad

2 C mixed field greens
1 large carrot, peeled and shredded
¼ C dried cranberry craisins
3 T raw pistachios

Arrange field greens in two large soup bowls. Place a mound of carrots in the center of the greens. Sprinkle craisins and pistachios on the greens around the carrots. Dress with raspberry vinaigrette dressing.

Yield: 2 large salads

NUTRI-NOTE:
The carrot gets its bright orange color from beta carotene, which is metabolized into vitamin A in humans. Carotenes help support immune function and neutralize destructive free radicals.

"If it's not food…don't eat it!"

Kelly Hayford, CNC

Cauliflower Salad Vinaigrette

1 ½ C diced cauliflower
1 C fresh sliced mushrooms
2 stalks celery
1 C julienned red pepper
¼ C raw pine nuts (optional)
¼ C extra virgin olive oil
¼ t sea salt
Dash pepper
2 T balsamic vinegar
¼ t dried oregano
¼ t dried basil
Dash tarragon
Dash garlic powder

Cut celery crosswise in thin slivers. Combine in small mixing bowl with cauliflower, mushrooms, and red pepper. In a separate bowl, mix together oil, salt, pepper, vinegar and spices. Pour over vegetables and toss well. Add pine nuts if desired.

Yield: 3 servings

NUTRI-NOTE:
Cauliflower contains allicin, which can improve heart health and reduce the risk of strokes.

*"Food is a powerful medicine,
probably the most powerful medicine
you will ever take."*

Barry Sears, MD

Cherry - Apple Salad with Maple Dressing

2 T extra virgin olive oil
2 T pure maple syrup
2 T apple cider vinegar
2 T arrowroot
6 C mixed spring greens
1 Granny Smith apple, peeled and cored
3/8 C dried cherries
3/8 C coarsely chopped walnuts

In a small bowl, mix oil, water, syrup and vinegar. Add arrowroot and whisk together until dressing is creamy. Set aside. Cut apple into matchstick strips. Place into mixing bowl and toss with greens, cherries and walnuts. Divide salad equally among plates. Drizzle dressing atop each salad and serve.

Yield: 3 servings

NUTRI-NOTE:
Cherries are rich in Vitamin C, contain antioxidants that neutralize free radicals, and provide melatonin, a natural pain reliever, inflammation inhibitor, and sleep aid.

"Where green plants cannot grow, we cannot live."

Udo Erasmus, PhD

Cool as a Cucumber Salad

2 C chopped cucumber
1/3 C diced red pepper
2 scallions thinly sliced
2 T fresh mint leaves, minced
2 t lemon juice
1 t extra virgin olive oil
2 t balsamic vinegar
Dash sea salt
Pinch pepper

In a small mixing bowl, combine cucumber, red pepper, scallions and mint. In a separate bowl, whisk together remaining ingredients. Toss with vegetables and serve.

Yield: 2 servings

TASTY TIP:
Substitute chopped red tomato for pepper.

*"Taste buds are creatures of habit –
and habits can be changed."*

Yolanda Bergman

Eggless Mayonnaise

1 T extra virgin olive oil
2 t apple cider vinegar
3 t pure maple syrup
3 T + 1 t tapioca starch
Pinch sea salt

Stir together all ingredients until creamy.

Yield: 1/4 C

TASTY TIP:
For mock hollandaise
sauce, add to basic
mayonnaise recipe 1 t
Dijon mustard, and a
smidge of pepper.
Thin with a few drops
of water.

"Nature…has been feeding humanity
for thousands of years without the least confusion."

Dr. John Douillard

Mango, Avocado and Black Bean Salad

1 firm but ripe avocado, peeled
1 firm but ripe mango, peeled
½ C finely diced red pepper
½ can (15 oz) black beans, drained and rinsed
1 T lemon or lime juice
1 T extra virgin olive oil
1 T chopped fresh cilantro
Dash sea salt
Pinch pepper
Dash stevia powder
2 large leaves Bibb or Boston lettuce

Dice avocado and mango into ½ inch cubes. Gently combine with 1 t lemon or lime juice in medium bowl, fold in peppers, and set aside. In a separate bowl, whisk together oil, remaining lemon juice, spices and seasonings. Add beans and toss. Place lettuce leaves in center of two small platters. Spoon black beans onto center of leaf, arrange mango/avocado mixture around beans, and serve.

Yield: 2 servings

NUTRI-NOTE:
Each colorful serving contains about 11 g of fiber and 9 g of protein.

Miso Salad Dressing

¼ C white miso
½ C extra virgin olive oil
1/6 C water
1/8 C apple cider vinegar
1/8 C wheat-free tamari
1/8 C finely chopped onion
1 clove garlic, crushed

Blend all ingredients together thoroughly. Chill before serving.

Yield: 1 C

NUTRI-NOTE:
Miso is a traditional enzyme-rich Japanese seasoning produced by fermenting rice, barley or soybeans.

*"The food giants have…
warped your food consciousness
to make you a willing participant
in your own demise."*

Paul Stitt

Nectarine Sunburst Salad

2 C baby arugula
2 ripe nectarines
8 soft pitted dates, coarsely chopped
1 T walnut oil
1 t apple cider vinegar
½ t pure maple syrup

Divide arugula and place in middle of two large salad plates. Cut nectarines to the pit to form about 10 thin slices each. Arrange nectarine slices, sunburst style, around the outside of each plate. Place dates in center atop arugula. In a small bowl, whisk together vinegar, oil and syrup. Drizzle dressing evenly around the arugula.

Yield: 2 servings

NUTRI-NOTE:
Nectarines are a good source of beta-carotene and are protective against epithelial cell cancers of the skin, lungs and throat.

"If man were to eat foods in their natural states, he certainly would not be subject to disease."

Satya Sai Baba

Nutty Slaw

3 C shredded green cabbage
3 C shredded red cabbage
2 C shredded carrots
¼ C slivered almonds
¼ C raw sunflower seeds
3 T extra virgin olive oil
3 T pure maple syrup
2 T apple cider vinegar
1/3 C tapioca starch
1 T Dijon mustard
¼ t celery seed
Dash black pepper

Place cabbage and carrot shreds into a large mixing bowl. Toss together with almonds and sunflower seeds. Set aside. Place tapioca into a small mixing bowl, add syrup, vinegar, mustard, and oil, and stir together until well blended. Pour into cabbage mixture and toss until slaw is well coated. Add pepper and celery seeds and incorporate thoroughly.

Yield: 6 servings

HELPFUL HINT:
To save time, use a 16-ounce bag of pre-shredded green and red cabbage.

Pear Salad with Arugula and Pecans

4 C baby arugula, rinsed, dried and packed tightly
2 ripe Bartlett pears
½ C pecan halves

Place greens on chilled salad plates. Peel and core pears. Cut lengthwise in narrow slices. Arrange pear slices on each plate of greens in a spoke-like design. Top each salad with 2 T pecans. Serve with raspberry vinaigrette dressing.

Yield: 4 servings

NUTRI-NOTE:
Pears are an excellent source of fiber and a good source of vitamin C.

*"If you strive for thin, you'll never win.
Strive for health and thin will follow."*

Elson Haas, MD

Pico de Gallo with Jicama

2 C raw jicama, peeled and diced
1 red pepper, seeded and chopped finely
½ medium onion, sliced very thinly
1 C cucumber, peeled and diced
¼ C extra virgin olive oil
2 T red wine vinegar
½ t oregano
1/8 t salt
1/8 t pepper

In a medium bowl, combine first four ingredients.
In a small bowl, mix oil, vinegar, oregano, salt and
pepper. Combine with vegetables and toss lightly.

Yield: 6 servings

NUTRI-NOTE:
Jicama is a sweet,
crunchy root high in
fiber and low in
calories.

*"Everything I've learned about food and health
can be summed up in seven words:
Eat food, not too much, mostly plants."*

Michael Pollan

Raspberry Dressing

¾ C fresh raspberries
1 T pure maple syrup
1 T apple cider vinegar
1 T lemon juice
1 t dried basil

Combine all ingredients in a blender until smooth.

Yield: ½ C

TASTY TIP:
For variety,
strawberries may
be substituted for
some or all of the
raspberries.

*"Drugs may change the blood chemistry,
but they cannot rebuild or replace tissue.
Only foods can do that."*

Dr. Bernard Jensen

Spinach Salad with Oranges

1 T orange juice
1 t balsamic vinegar
½ t tapioca flour
1/8 t sea salt
4 C baby spinach leaves
1 C radicchio shreds
1 clementine, peeled
2 T raw pine nuts

Combine orange juice, vinegar, flour, and salt. Mix well and set aside. Place spinach and radicchio into salad bowl. Separate sections of clementine and cut into bite-sized pieces. Add clementine and dressing to spinach and toss well. Sprinkle with pine nuts.

Yield: 2 servings

HELPFUL HINT:
To save time, use an 11-oz can of mandarin oranges, drained, in place of clementine.

"What passes through the mouth passes all understanding."

Anonymous

Spring Salad with Sprouts

2 C mixed spring greens
1 ripe avocado
7 oz jar roasted red peppers, drained
½ small zucchini
½ C lentil, chick pea or mung sprouts, rinsed well

In a mixing bowl, mash avocado. Dice red peppers and incorporate with avocado. Place greens on serving plate. Slice zucchini crosswise in thin slices and arrange evenly around perimeter. Scoop avocado mixture into center of greens and arrange sprouts around plate. Drizzle with vinaigrette dressing (see below).

Yield: 2 servings

NUTRI-NOTE:
Avocados have beneficial fatty acids and are excellent sources of plant-based protein.

"A seed when planted will sprout into life…
but when cooked, the life is destroyed."

Satya Sai Baba

Vinaigrette Dressing

3 T extra virgin olive oil
1 T balsamic vinegar
2 t Dijon mustard
½ t minced garlic
½ t dried rosemary, ground

In a small bowl, combine oil, vinegar, mustard, garlic and rosemary and stir well. Drizzle over mixed green salad.

Yield: ¼ C

HELPFUL HINT: In purchasing balsamic vinegar, check the label to rule out sulfites. Not all balsamic vinegars have sulfites, but many less expensive choices do.

"Wholesome food is one of the causes of the growth of living beings....
Unwholesome food is one of the causes of the growth of diseases."

Charaka

Waldorf Salad

2 sweet red apples, cored and diced
½ C seedless red grapes, halved
1 stalk celery, diced
½ C walnuts, chopped
4 T vanilla flavored almond milk
½ t vanilla extract

Toss all ingredients together in a medium serving bowl. Serve chilled.

Yield: 4 servings

NUTRI-NOTE: Apple skins contain triterpenoids, natural compounds with potent anti-cancer activity that are particularly protective against human liver, colon and breast cancer cell growth.

"An apple a day keeps the doctor away."

Proverb

ENTREES & SIDES

Artichoke and Spinach Casserole

20 oz chopped frozen spinach, defrosted
1 can small artichoke hearts in water, halved
1 C Daiya mozzarella shreds
12 oz So Delicious vanilla-flavored coconut milk
   yogurt
1 medium onion, diced
2 cloves garlic, minced
2 T cold-pressed extra virgin olive oil

Preheat oven to 350 F. In a colander, drain and press spinach. Set aside. Saute onions in 1 T oil for 3 minutes, stirring frequently. Add garlic and sauté 1 minute more. In a large bowl, combine spinach, onions and yogurt. Lightly grease a 2 quart baking dish with remaining oil and fill with spinach mixture. Cover with artichoke halves, flat side down. Top with mozzarella shreds and bake for 30 minutes. Serve hot.

Yield: 8 servings

NUTRI-NOTE:
Artichokes help lower cholesterol and blood sugar and stimulate bile flow.

"The preparation and refinement of food products either entirely eliminates or in part destroys the vital elements in the original material."

US Department of Agriculture

Baked Carrots

1 lb carrots, peeled and thinly sliced
½ C unfiltered apple juice
¼ C raisins
¼ C sliced raw almonds
1 T lemon juice
2 t ground cinnamon
¼ t nutmeg
Dash ginger powder

Preheat oven to 375 degrees. In a mixing bowl, thoroughly combine carrots, apple juice, raisins, lemon juice and spices. Transfer to a 1.5 qt baking dish. Bake uncovered for 40 minutes, stirring liquid up to the top every 10 minutes. Remove from oven, stir in almonds, and serve.

Yield: 8 servings

NUTRI-NOTE: Researchers have found that falcarinol, a natural compound in carrots that protects from fungal diseases that cause black spots on the roots during storage, could also help prevent cancer.

*"Nothing will benefit health
and increase the chances for survival on earth
as the evolution of a vegetarian diet."*

Albert Einstein

Black Beans with Rice

1 can (15 oz) black beans
½ medium onion, chopped
1 clove garlic, minced
1 t ground coriander
1 ½ t ground cumin
1 t extra virgin olive oil
½ t sea salt
Pinch cayenne pepper
1 ½ t lemon juice
2 C cooked brown rice

In a large soup pot, saute onion and garlic in oil
5-6 minutes. Add beans , coriander, cumin, salt,
cayenne, and lemon juice and incorporate well.
Cook about 10 minutes over medium heat,
stirring frequently. Arrange beans over brown
rice and serve.

Yield: 4 servings

NUTRI-NOTE:
Brown rice is high in
B vitamins, and also
contains iron, vitamin
E, and protein.

"Don't dig your grave with your own knife and fork."

English Proverb

Carrot Parsnip Risotto

3 C water
2T extra virgin olive oil
1 large onion, diced
¼ t sea salt
1 large or 2 small parsnips, finely sliced
1 large or 2 small carrots, finely sliced
2/3 C Arborio rice
2 oz vegetable broth
1T parsley, finely minced

Heat oil in large cooking pot over medium heat. Add onion and a pinch of salt and sauté until limp, about 2 minutes. Stir in parsnips and carrots and sauté 1 minute more. Stir in rice, gradually adding broth and stirring very frequently. Cook about 25 minutes until liquid is absorbed into the rice. Stir in minced parsley and serve immediately.

Yield: 3 servings

HELPFUL HINT: If rice begins to boil, reduce heat. If necessary, add additional hot water ¼ C at a time. Finished risotto should be creamy but not soupy.

"Our own physical body possesses a wisdom
which we who inhabit the body lack.
We give it orders which make no sense."

Henry Miller

Cauliflower Mashed Potatoes

1 head cauliflower
2 oz So Delicious coconut milk
½ t sea salt
¼ t stevia powder
Fresh ground pepper to taste

Remove leaves and stalk from cauliflower. Steam in steamer basket for 35-40 minutes until very soft. Place all ingredients in food processor and process until thoroughly blended.

Yield: 4 servings

NUTRI-NOTE: Cauliflower contains selenium, an antioxidant mineral that works well with vitamin C to strengthen the immune system.

"We call a section in our local supermarket the 'Health Food Section.'
What is the rest of the store called,
the 'Death and Disease Section'?"

Carol Simontacchi

Coconut Curry Quinoa Stew

2 T extra virgin olive oil
1 medium leek, thinly sliced crosswise
1 small zucchini, cubed
1 medium carrot, peeled and sliced into thin
   pennies
2 ribs celery, diced
½ small yellow pepper, diced
2 t curry powder
1 t ground cumin
1 C uncooked quinoa
1 C water
½ t sea salt
Dash black pepper
1 cinnamon stick
2/3 C cooked chickpeas
1 ½ C light coconut milk
¼ C raisins (optional)

In a deep stew pot add olive oil and leek and cook
for 2 minutes over medium heat, stirring often.
Add carrots and cook 2 minutes more. Stir in all
of the other ingredients, cover, and simmer about
30 minutes, stirring frequently. Remove
cinnamon stick and serve.

Yield: 4 servings

NUTRI-NOTE:
Quinoa is a prized ancient
Incan grain providing all
eight essential amino acids.
Curry and its active
ingredient turmeric are
much more easily absorbed
in the presence of black
pepper.

Creamed Spinach

10 oz bag frozen chopped spinach, defrosted and
   drained
2 medium shallots, minced
1 large clove garlic, minced
2 t extra virgin olive oil
2 T raw pine nuts
2 T salba (chia) seeds, finely ground
1/8 t salt
1/8 t pepper
1/8 t nutmeg
1 C So Delicious vanilla-flavored coconut milk
¼ t stevia powder

In a food processor, combine pine nuts, salba,
and ¼ C coconut milk until well blended. Set
aside. In a medium saucepan, sauté shallots in oil
over medium heat for 1 minute. Add garlic and
sauté 1 minute more. Add spinach, salt, pepper,
nutmeg, stevia, pine nut mixture and remaining
coconut milk. Cook 5 minutes, stirring frequently,
and serve.

Yield: 4 servings

*"You are what you eat.
And you are also what you don't eat."*

Anonymous

Escarole with Garlic and Walnuts

1 head escarole
1 t extra virgin olive oil
¼ C raisins
¼ C diced red pepper
1T chopped walnuts
2 large cloves garlic, minced
2 oz vegetable broth
Pinch sea salt

Remove escarole leaves from head, wash
thoroughly, and pat dry. Tear into 2 inch pieces
and set aside.   Heat oil in large soup pot over
medium high heat. Add garlic and pepper and
sauté 2 minutes, stirring constantly. Add broth,
escarole, raisins, walnuts, and salt and cook
about 3 minutes until escarole is wilted and liquid
is absorbed.

Yield: 3 servings

*"Diet is the essential key to all successful healing.
Without a proper balanced diet, the effectiveness
of herbal treatment is very limited."*

Michael Tierra, CA, ND

Green Beans with Shallots

3/4 lb fresh whole green beans, trimmed
1 T extra virgin olive oil
2 shallots, chopped
3 cloves garlic, diced
1 t dried parsley
½ t dried oregano
Salt and pepper to taste

Steam beans in steamer basket until just tender, about 5 minutes. Remove from heat. Heat oil in large fry pan over medium heat. Add shallots and cook, stirring occasionally, until soft and golden. Add garlic and cook one more minute. Place green beans into pan. Add parsley, oregano, salt and pepper and toss gently to coat. Transfer to serving platter and serve.

Yield: 4 servings

NUTRI-NOTE:
Shallots appear to contain more cancer-protective antioxidants known as flavonoids and phenols than other members of the onion family.

"Almost every human malady is connected...with the stomach."

Sir Francis Head

Green Beans with Tomatoes

1 ½ lbs green beans, trimmed
¼ C extra virgin olive oil
10 cloves garlic, thinly sliced
1 C cherry or grape tomatoes, halved
3/4 t salt
½ t black pepper
¼ t oregano
¼ t thyme
½ C vegetable broth

Cut beans into approximately 2 inch lengths. Place in steamer basket and steam until just tender, about 5 minutes. Remove from steamer and set aside. Heat oil in skillet over medium high heat. Add garlic and cook 1 minute, stirring frequently. Add tomatoes and seasonings and cook 2 minutes, continuing to stir. Stir in broth and beans and cook 2 to 3 minutes more.

Yield: 6 servings

"Health depends upon nutrition
more than on any other single factor."

Dr. William Sebrell

Moroccan Stew

1 ½ C water
1 large onion, finely chopped
2 large red peppers, seeded and chopped
3 garlic cloves, minced
1 T pure maple syrup
1 t ground coriander
½ t cinnamon
½ t ground cumin
½ t ginger
½ t vanilla extract
2 medium yams or sweet potatoes, peeled and
    cut into ½ inch cubes
1 can (15 oz) diced tomatoes
1 can (15 oz) chickpeas, drained and rinsed
½ t sea salt
Dash pepper
¼ C raisins (optional)

Heat ¼ C of water in a soup pot over medium
heat. Add onion, peppers, and garlic, and cook
for 5 minutes, stirring occasionally. Stir in the
maple syrup, coriander, cinnamon, cumin, ginger
and vanilla and cook for 1 minute, stirring
constantly. Add potatoes, tomatoes, chickpeas,
remaining water and craisins, if desired. Bring to
a boil, then reduce heat to low. Simmer, covered,
for 30 minutes or until potatoes are tender.
Season with salt and pepper. Serve over a bed of
quinoa or brown rice.

Yield: 6 servings

Oat and Apple Delight

2 C water
½ C oat bran
¼ t cinnamon
½ C dates, pitted and chopped
½ C walnuts, chopped
1 red apple, peeled and grated
½ C vanilla flavored almond milk

Bring water to a boil. Add oat bran and cinnamon, stirring frequently. Reduce heat to medium and cook until liquid is absorbed (about 3 minutes). Stir in dates, walnuts and apple. Separate into bowls. Pour ¼ C almond milk atop each bowl and serve.

Yield: 2 generous servings

NUTRI-NOTE:
Oat bran is rich in a soluble fiber called beta-glucan. In 1997, the U.S. Food and Drug Administration passed a unique ruling that allowed oat bran to be registered as the first cholesterol-reducing food.

"One should eat to live, not live to eat."

Cicero

Orange Quinoa Pilaf

2 C vegetable stock
1 C uncooked quinoa
1 C grated carrots
2 large oranges, peeled and cut into small chunks
1 t dried orange peel
¼ C raisins
¼ t sea salt
¼ t ground cinnamon

In a large saucepan, bring broth and quinoa to a
boil. Stir in carrots, oranges, orange peel, raisins,
salt and cinnamon and return to boil. Reduce
heat to medium-low and simmer, covered, about
10 minutes or until all liquid is absorbed.

Yield: 4 servings

HELPFUL HINT:
For a shortcut,
use a 12-oz can
of drained
mandarin
oranges in place
of fresh oranges.

*"Most patients never heard a word
from their doctor regarding their diet.
It is much easier to give in and treat the symptoms
...than to sit and discuss lifestyle changes."*

Ana Negron, MD

Pad Thai

8 oz Asian rice noodles
4 cloves garlic, minced
2 scallions, thinly sliced
1 shallot, minced
2 C fresh mung bean sprouts
¼ C Sucanat or raw cane sugar
¼ C dry roasted unsalted peanuts, ground
2 T coconut oil
2 T wheat-free tamari
2 T creamy peanut butter
2 T lemon juice
2 T vegetable stock
1 t tamarind paste
1 t chili sauce
1 T arrowroot

In a large soup pot, bring about 8 cups of water
to a boil. Remove from heat, add noodles, and
soak for 8 minutes. Drain, rinse with cold water,
and set aside. Place arrowroot into a small mixing
bowl. Gradually stir in tamari, peanut butter,
lemon juice, chili sauce, vegetable stock,
tamarind paste, and Sucanat and mix thoroughly.
In a large wok, sauté shallot and garlic in coconut
oil for 2 minutes over medium heat. Add cooked
noodles and tamari mixture, stir well, and cook for
3 minutes. Add bean sprouts and toss to coat.
Transfer to serving dish, sprinkle with ground
peanuts, top with scallions, and serve
immediately.

Yield: 2 servings

Pasta with Cannellini and Broccoli

16 oz bag frozen broccoli florets
8 oz rice penne pasta
2 t extra virgin olive oil
3 ribs of celery, diced
1 medium onion, diced
3 cloves garlic, minced
1 tsp oregano
1/8 t sea salt
1 C tomato sauce
16 oz can cannellini beans, drained

Bring water to boil and steam broccoli for about 6 minutes. Cook pasta according to package directions. Drain and set aside. In a large pot, heat oil. Add onion and celery and saute 2 minutes, stirring frequently. Add garlic, oregano and sea salt and sauté one minute more. Add pasta sauce and drained beans and cook another minute. Fold in pasta and toss well. Put into a large casserole dish and top with broccoli .

Yield: 4-6 servings.

*"The body intuitively knows
exactly what foods are truly best for it.
We simply must learn to be better listeners."*

Mark Percival

Pepper and Zucchini Stir Fry

1 medium onion
1 sweet red pepper, seeded
1 medium zucchini
2 T extra virgin olive oil
½ t minced garlic
Sea salt and pepper to taste

Thinly slice onion into rings, then halve and separate rings. Cut pepper and zucchini lengthwise in 1/4 inch strips about 2 inches long. Pat dry. Saute onions in oil over medium-high heat until soft and translucent, stirring frequently. Add peppers and zucchini and sauté 3-4 minutes more, stirring as before. Add garlic and cook 2 more minutes. Season with salt and pepper to taste. Serve with brown rice or quinoa.

Yield: 4 servings

"Food is a living miracle.
Your body is a living miracle.
Eat at the same level of miracle that you are."

Grace Parusha

Sauteed Baby Spinach

2 T extra virgin olive oil
4 medium garlic cloves, thinly sliced
¼ C raisins
¼ C vegetable broth
1 lb fresh baby spinach
¼ t salt
¼ t pepper
2 t organic raw blue agave (optional)

Heat oil in a large pot. Add garlic and sauté 1 minute. Add raisins and broth and cook 2 minutes. Add spinach and cook for about 3 minutes, stirring frequently, until wilted. Season with salt and pepper, drizzle with agave if desired, and serve.

Yield: 4 servings

NUTRI-NOTE:
Calcium is abundant in green leafy vegetables like spinach.

"Our most powerful weapon against cancer is the food we eat every day."

T. Colin Campbell, PhD

Sauteed Beet Greens

Bunch fresh beet greens, washed, and stemmed
1 T extra virgin olive oil
1 medium onion, diced

Cut greens into ½ inch strips, then crosswise to 2 inches in length. In large fry pan or wok, sauté onion over medium high heat about 4 minutes or until translucent and golden. Add greens and stir with wooden spoon continuously about 1 minute more until just wilted.

Yield: 2-3 servings

NUTRI-NOTE: Containing a larger amount of nutrients than beet root, beet greens are rich in iron, calcium, vitamin A, folic acid, manganese, potassium, and fiber.

"If I were asked to design a diet today that promoted the development of cancer to the maximum, I couldn't improve on our present diet!"

Richard Beliveau, PhD

Sesame Noodles

8 oz brown rice linguine or 100% buckwheat soba
2 T apple cider vinegar
2 T wheat-free tamari
2 T raw almond butter
1 T raw tahini (sesame butter)
1 T peanut butter
1 T extra virgin olive oil
1 t organic raw blue agave nectar
½ t sesame oil

Cook pasta according to package directions until al dente. Drain, rinse, and mix with olive oil in serving bowl, stirring well to coat. Combine all remaining ingredients in a small bowl, mixing until smooth. Pour over pasta and toss to coat. Serve at room temperature.

Yield: 3 servings

NUTRI-NOTE: Buckwheat provides nearly twice the amount of protein found in rice and contains high amounts of rutin, an antioxidant bioflavonoid not found in other grains or beans.

*"If you are what you eat,
why would you want to be a Twinkie or a hot dog?"*

Gary Null, PhD

Snap Peas with Roasted Peppers

3 C fresh snap pea pods
½ C roasted red peppers, drained and diced
1 t fresh lemon juice
1 t extra virgin olive oil
¼ t sea salt
Pinch pepper
¼ t dried oregano
¼ t garlic powder (optional)

Steam pea pods in steamer basket about 7 minutes or until tender. Place all remaining ingredients into a medium bowl and stir. Add peas, toss well and serve.

Yield: 4 servings

NUTRI-NOTE: Colorful peppers are high in carotenoids and vitamin C, but as members of the nightshade family they are best avoided by persons with rheumatoid arthritis.

*"To eat is a necessity,
but to eat intelligently is an art."*

La Rochefoucauld

Spicy Roasted Sweet Potatoes

2 medium yams or sweet potatoes, peeled
1T coconut oil
½ t cinnamon
½ t sea salt
¼ t Sucanat or dehydrated cane juice
¼ t ground cumin

Preheat oven to 450 degrees. Cut potatoes into ½ inch strips. Place oil in large bowl and stir in potato wedges until well coated. Pour seasonings into plastic bag. Add potatoes, seal bag, and shake thoroughly. Place potatoes on baking sheet without overlapping. Bake for 20 minutes, turning once half way through.

Yield: 3-4 servings

NUTRI-NOTE: This dish is loaded with cancer-fighting beta-carotene.

"What we eat has changed more in the last forty years than in the previous forty thousand."

Eric Schlosser

Sweet Potato Stew

1 large onion, chopped
4 cloves garlic, chopped
15-oz. can great Northern beans, rinsed and
   drained
14-oz can diced tomatoes
2 stalks celery, finely chopped
½ lb sweet potatoes, peeled and chopped
6 oz kale, stripped from stalks and thinly sliced
4 oz mushrooms, chopped
2/3 C vegetable broth
¼ C dry red wine
1 t Liquid Smoke
1 t salt
1 t dried rosemary
1 t dried thyme
1 t dried basil
¼ t ground black pepper

Steam fry onion and garlic in a deep soup pot
over medium heat until soft, adding water by the
teaspoon as needed to prevent sticking. Add kale
and stir for 1 minute more. Add remaining
ingredients and simmer, covered, for 1 hour.
Serve with whole grain bread or brown rice.

Yield: 4-6 servings

*"We are indeed much more than what we eat,
but what we eat can nevertheless help us
to be much more than what we are."*

Alice May Brock

Swiss Chard with Raisins and Pine Nuts

1 ½ lbs Swiss chard (preferably red)
½ C raw pine nuts
¼ C extra virgin olive oil
1 medium onion, finely chopped
½ C golden raisins
1 C water
1 t maple syrup
Salt and pepper to taste

Tear chard leaves from stems, then coarsely chops stems and leaves separately. Cook onion in oil, stirring occasionally, 1 minute. Add chard stems and cook 2 minutes, stirring as before. Add raisins and ½ C water and simmer, covered, about 3 minutes until stems are softened. Add chard leaves, pine nuts and remaining water and simmer 3 minutes more, stirring occasionally, until leaves are tender. Stir in maple syrup and season with salt and pepper.

Yield: 4 servings

NUTRI-NOTE: Research has shown that chard leaves contain at least 13 different polyphenol antioxidants, including kaempferol, the cardioprotective flavonoid, and syringic acid, known for its blood sugar regulating properties.

Vegetarian Chili

1 ½ cans (15 oz each) red kidney beans
1 ½ C chopped onions
3 cloves garlic, minced
1 T extra virgin olive oil
2 C canned crushed red tomatoes
2 T tomato paste
2 T paprika
1 ½ t chili powder
1 t dried basil
1 t dried oregano
½ t cumin

Saute onion and garlic in olive oil until onions are translucent. Add tomatoes, beans and seasonings. Simmer for one hour, stirring occasionally, adding water when necessary to maintain consistency. Serve over a bed of brown rice.

Yield: 4-5 hearty servings

TASTY TIP:
For variety, roll into brown rice or organiz corn tortillas.

"The Chinese do not draw any distinction between food and medicine."

Lin Yutang

Zucchini Apple Pancakes

1 medium zucchini, grated
1 medium red apple, cored and shredded
½ C oat bran
¼ C water
¼ C onion, finely diced
1 T salba (chia), ground
1 T extra virgin olive oil
½ t sea salt
¼ t lemon juice
Dash black pepper

Preheat oven to 450 degrees. In a small bowl, mix together the salba and water and set aside. In a medium bowl, combine the zucchini, apple, lemon juice, onions, salt and pepper. Add salba mixture and stir well. Slowly add the oat bran, stirring until uniformly moist. Spread olive oil evenly on baking pan. Form batter into approximately 2 inch round patties about ½ inch thick. Bake 8 minutes on each side until slightly browned.

Yield: 8-10 pancakes

NUTRI-NOTE:
Zucchini is rich in organic sodium, an alkaline element that helps to neutralize acid and restore a sodium-exhausted liver.

"Our own physical body possesses a wisdom which we who inhabit the body lack. We give it orders which make no sense."

Henry Miller

Zucchini Spaghetti and Sauce

1 medium-large zucchini squash, scrubbed
1 C tomato sauce
1 large garlic clove, minced
½ t dried oregano
½ t dried basil
3 T Daiya mozzarella style shreds

Shred squash in food processor. Set aside. Put tomato sauce, garlic, oregano, and basil into sauce pan and heat for 8 minutes. Pour over zucchini "noodles" and sprinkle shredded "cheese" over top.

Yield: 3 servings

NUTRI-NOTE: Daiya vegan shreds are made entirely from plant-based ingredients and are free of cholesterol, trans-fats, soy, and gluten.

"The way you do food is the way you do life."

Jerrol Kimmel, RN, MA

SWEETS & TREATS

Almond Cookies

2 C almond meal flour
½ C raw almond butter
6 T pure maple syrup
1 t vanilla extract
1 t almond extract
2 T slivered almonds

Preheat oven to 350 degrees. Place all ingredients except slivered almonds into food processor and process thoroughly, stopping occasionally to scrape sides of bowl. Transfer dough to a mixing bowl and knead until uniformly moist. Form dough into balls and press into cookies no more than ½ inch high and 2 inches wide. Place onto foil baking pan and press a few almond slivers into the top of each cookie. Bake 12 minutes. Remove from oven, allow to cool, and store in an airtight container.

Yield: 16 cookies

NUTRI-NOTE:
One ounce of raw almonds provides 35% of the RDA for vitamin E, 3 grams of fiber, and 75 mg of calcium.

"Food is an important part of a balanced diet."

Fran Liebowitz

Almond Sesame Halvah

1 ½ C raw almonds
½ C raw tahini (sesame butter)
¼ C brown rice syrup
2 T flaxseeds, ground
1 ½ T raw blue organic agave nectar
½ t vanilla extract
½ t almond extract

In a food processor, process almonds until finely ground. Add all of the other ingredients and process thoroughly. Press onto a large plate until mixture is about ½ inch thick. Chill in refrigerator for one hour or more. Cut into inch square pieces.

Yield: 32 pieces

TASTY TIP:
Agave nectar is made from the blue agave cactus plant. Because its sugars are about 90% fructose, which is sweeter than sugar, use it sparingly, only half as much as you would sugar.

*"The road to good health
is paved with good intestines."*

Anonymous

Asian Pear Salad

1 Asian pear
1 red apple
2 stalks of celery
12 pitted dates
2 ripe bananas
1 T raw blue organic agave nectar
1 T lemon juice

Dice pear, apple, and celery. Place into medium bowl. Chop dates, add to bowl, and set aside. In food processor, puree bananas, agave, and lemon juice. Add to fruit bowl and toss well. Serve chilled.

Yield: 4 servings

TASTY TIP:
Any pear can be used in this salad, but while European pears have soft melting textures, Asian pears are very firm and crisp, as well as juicy and sweet.

"Too many of us health care professionals ignore the connections between nutrition and health. We treat the symptoms ... with hardly a word about the person's food choices."

Ana Negron, MD

Banana Almond Pie

2 C raw almonds
1 T water
¼ C brown rice syrup
18 pitted dates
2¼ t vanilla
4 ripe medium bananas
1 C So Delicious vanilla-flavored coconut milk
Dash sea salt
1 t lemon juice
2 T ground white chia seeds
½ C unsweetened shredded coconut
1 T pure maple syrup

Place almonds in food processor and grind to powder. Add water, rice syrup, 8 dates and ¼ t vanilla and process about 30 seconds until mixture is pasty. Press into 8 inch pie tin and set aside. In a blender, place 3 of the bananas, 10 dates, and the rest of the vanilla. Add all of the remaining ingredients and blend on low speed until creamy, pausing the blender and scraping the jar sides as necessary. Pour contents into pie tin and freeze for at least 2 hours. Before serving, halve the last banana lengthwise and widthwise and arrange slices, cut side down, on top of pie. Store uneaten pie in freezer and allow to defrost slightly (about 20 minutes) before slicing.

Yield: 1 pie, about 8 slices

TASTY TIP:
For variety, replace banana topping with 3 sliced strawberries.

Banana Nut Pudding

2 C pecans, soaked in water for 6 hours and
   drained
2 ripe bananas
1 ½ C pitted dates
2 t vanilla
1 t maple syrup
2 t salba, ground
¼ water
1 t cinnamon (optional)
4 pecan halves

Process all ingredients except 4 pecan halves in
a food processor until smooth. Spoon into
dessert bowls. Press pecan half into top of each
portion. Serve chilled.

Yield: 4 filling servings

NUTRI-NOTE:
Because of their
potassium and
tryptophane content,
bananas are good for
your heart and nerves
and can act as mood
enhancers or mild
sedatives.

*"Tell me what you eat,
and I will tell you who you are."*

Jean Anthelme Brillat-Savarin

Candy Cane Parfait

1 frozen banana, slightly defrosted, cut into small chunks
½ C frozen raspberries
¾ C So Delicious vanilla-flavored coconut milk yogurt
¼ C unsweetened apple juice
4 T salba, ground
2 T chopped walnuts
¼ t stevia
½ t pure almond extract

Mix yogurt well with 2 T salba. Set aside. Process banana, raspberries, and apple juice with ice crusher function. Add almond flavoring, stevia, and 2 T salba and blend just until smooth. Using a tablespoon, alternately layer ½ inch raspberry and yogurt mixtures into 6 oz-parfait glasses. Sprinkle 1 T nuts on top of each parfait. Refrigerate or serve immediately.

Yield: 2 yummy desserts

TASTY TIP:
Top with a fresh raspberry instead of nuts.

"The most basic weapons in the fight against disease are those most ignored by modern medicine: the numerous nutrients that the cells of our bodies need."

Dr. Roger Williams

Carob Mint Balls

8 soft dates, pitted
3 T raw blue organic agave nectar
½ t coconut oil
¾ C raw almond butter
3 T carob powder
2 T ground salba
2 dashes peppermint oil
¾ C chopped walnuts
1 T shredded unsweetened coconut
1T hempseeds or sesame seeds
1T finely chopped raw almonds or peanuts

In a food processor, combine dates, agave, oils, almond butter, carob, and salba until thoroughly blended, pausing to scrape bowl sides as necessary. Transfer to a mixing bowl. Add walnuts and knead dough manually until nuts are well incorporated. Form into tight 1 inch balls. Place coconut, seeds, and remaining nuts into separate piles on wax paper. Roll 5 balls in coconut until coated. Roll 5 balls in seeds until coated. Roll 5 balls in nuts until coated. Leave remaining 5 balls uncoated. Arrange on dessert serving platter and refrigerate.

Yield: 20 yummy pieces

HELPFUL HINT:
Make sure almond butter is well homogenized itself before mixing it with other ingredients.

Chocolate Dipped Strawberries

12 medium or 8 large strawberries with leaves
1.3 oz bar bittersweet dark chocolate

Line a baking tray with waxed paper. Wash strawberries and pat dry. In a small pot, melt chocolate slowly over low medium-low heat for about 15 seconds, stirring constantly. When fully melted, remove from heat. Pick up strawberries by the stem end one at a time and use a teaspoon to paint berry tip with chocolate. Set berry onto baking tray, leaf side down and chocolate side up. Repeat until all berries are coated. Refrigerate at least one hour.

NUTRI-NOTE:
Studies indicate that the flavonol antioxidants abundant in dark bittersweet chocolate help protect against heart disease, asthma, diabetes, and cancers of the lung, prostate, and skin.

"There is nothing in the world like chocolate. It is luxurious, sensuous, delightful, passionate, inspirational, sexual and exciting to all senses."

David Wolfe

Chocolate Crisp Brownies

½ C brown rice syrup
½ C raw almond butter
¼ C semi-sweet dark chocolate chips
1 C crispy brown rice cereal

In a medium bowl, stir together syrup and almond butter until creamy. Set aside. Heat chocolate chips in a small pot over medium heat, stirring constantly until just melted. Add to almond butter mixture and mix well. Stir in crispy rice until well incorporated. Press into 8 by 5 by 1 inch brownie pan and refrigerate 1-2 hours until firm. Cut into squares with a sharp knife, serve immediately, and return remaining portion to refrigerator.

Yield: 1 dozen brownies

HELPFUL HINT:
If oil has risen to the top of the almond butter jar, pour off before preparing recipe.

"There are four basic food groups: milk chocolate, dark chocolate, white chocolate, and chocolate truffles."

Anonymous

Date Nut Logs

1 ½ C pitted dates
1 C pecans
1 ¼ C unsweetened coconut shreds
1 t cinnamon
1 t vanilla

Soak dates in enough water to cover them for about 30 minutes. Drain. In a food processor, chop nuts until finely chopped. Add 1 C coconut, cinnamon, and vanilla, and process briefly. Add dates a few at a time, processing until well mixed. Transfer to a large bowl and knead well. Roll mixture tightly into finger-shaped 3-inch long logs. Roll in remaining coconut. Refrigerate.

Yield: About 20 logs

HELPFUL HINT: Double the recipe: While these will keep in the refrigerator for up to 2 weeks, your family will finish them off a lot sooner!

"It's bizarre that the produce manager is more important to my children's health than the pediatrician."

Meryl Streep

Flourless Carob Raspberry Torte

3 C raw walnuts
16 pitted dates
1 t stevia powder
¼ t sea salt
½ C unsweetened carob powder
½ t coconut oil
1 t vanilla extract
4 t water
2 T unsweetened raspberry preserves
8 large fresh raspberries

Place walnuts in food processor and process until finely ground. Add dates, stevia, salt, carob, oil, vanilla and water and process thoroughly until mixture sticks together. Transfer to flat serving plate and form into 6 inch round torte. Spread top with thin layer of preserves. Place raspberries evenly around torte, clock-like fashion, about 1 inch from perimeter. Chill for 2 hours before serving.

Yield: 8 rich servings

HELPFUL HINT: This decadent dessert will keep for 3 days in the refrigerator, but once you serve it there won't be any left to put back in.

Frangipane Custard

3/4 C almond meal
3/4 C vanilla-flavored almond milk
3 T pure maple syrup
2 T ground white chia seeds
1 1/2 t vanilla extract
2 large raspberries

Using a food processor or blender, combine all ingredients except raspberries until smooth and creamy. Transfer to small dessert bowls, top with raspberries, and chill in refrigerator for several hours.

Yield: 2 servings

"The kitchen is the great laboratory of the household, and much of the 'weal and woe' as far as regards bodily health, depends on the nature of the preparations concocted within its walls."

Isabella Beeton

Fruit Squares

3 C soft pitted dates
2 C dried cherries
1 C dark raisins
2 C hulled hempseeds
4 C walnuts

Grind walnuts in food processor until uniformly
chopped but not pulverized.   Set aside about 1/3.
Add fruit and hemp and process until well blended
(mixture will be very thick). Press into a 9 inch
square pan. Spread remaining walnuts on top
and press firmly into fruit mixture. Refrigerate at
least 1 hour. Cut into squares and serve.

Yield: 16 filling squares

HELPFUL HINT:
If dates are hard,
soak in water for
a few hours, and
drain well.

*"The power of food to harm or heal
has been largely overlooked by medical practitioners
– and consequently medical consumers alike."*

Susan Silberstein, PhD

Fudge Swirl Sundae

4 t carob powder
2 t hot water
¼ t vanilla extract
1 t stevia powder
4 ripe bananas, frozen
3 T chopped walnuts
2 T semi-sweet chocolate chips
Dash peppermint extract (optional)

In a small bowl, thoroughly stir together carob powder, stevia, vanilla, water, and peppermint (if desired). Set aside. Pass the bananas through a Champion Juicer using the solid plate. Gently swirl in the carob mixture. Spoon the soft ice cream into dessert bowls and top with nuts and chocolate chips. Serve immediately.

Yield: 2 servings

"I would cook dinner, but I can't find the can opener!"

Anonymous

Kiwi Strawberry Salad

2 kiwis, soft to touch
3 large strawberries
1 T lemon juice
1 T organic blue agave nectar
2 T orange juice
1 t vanilla
2 fresh mint leaves

Rinse strawberries and pat dry. Remove leaves.
Cut strawberries lengthwise into ¼ inch slices.
Using the point of a sharp paring knife, remove
ends of kiwis and peel. Cut crosswise into ¼ inch
slices. Arrange fruit in overlapping layers in small
dessert bowls. In a small bowl, mix lemon, agave,
orange juice and vanilla and drizzle over fruit.
Garnish with a mint leaf.

Yield: 2 servings

NUTRI-NOTE:
This refreshing dessert
provides over 200 mg
of vitamin C.

*"The body is a self-healing machine
when you supply it with an optimal
nutritional environment."*

Joel Fuhrman, MD

Mango Blueberry Cobbler

4 C ripe mango, cut in ½ inch chunks
1 C blueberries
1 C quinoa flakes
1 C rolled oats (gluten free)
¾ C brown rice flour
¾ C chopped walnuts
1 ½ tsp cinnamon
½ tsp nutmeg
½ C + 2 T Sucanat
½ C maple syrup
½ C coconut oil
1/3 C orange juice
Pinch sea salt

Spread half the mango chunks in a 2 quart oblong glass pan; dot with half the blueberries. Sprinkle 1 T Sucanat over the fruit. In a bowl, mix ½ C Sucanat with the quinoa flakes, oats, rice flour, walnuts, cinnamon, and nutmeg. Add the oil and maple syrup and mix well. Spread half this mixture over the layer of fruit, add the remaining mangoes and berries, sprinkle with the remaining Sucanat, and cover with the rest of the syrup mixture. Pour the orange juice evenly over the top. Bake at 375 F for 30 minutes. Spoon out and serve warm.

Yield: 8 servings.

HELPFUL HINT:
To liquefy solid coconut oil, immerse jar in warm water for several minutes.

Nut Torte

½ C raw cashews
½ C raw almonds
½ C raw Brazil nuts
½ C raw sunflower seeds
1 C soft pitted dates
2 T raw organic blue agave nectar
1 t unsweetened shredded coconut

Grind nuts and seeds in food processor until finely ground. Transfer to a mixing bowl. Process together dates and agave thoroughly, scraping sides of bowl and reprocessing until mixture is a smooth paste. Add nuts back into paste and re-process until well mixed. Place onto serving plate, moisten hands, and shape mixture into 6 inch round torte. Sprinkle with coconut and press onto top of cake. Refrigerate a few hours before serving.

Yield: 8 servings

HELPFUL HINT:
If dates are hard, soak overnight and drain.

"Children's diseases are parents' mistakes."

Herbert Shelton

Peach Wheel with Cherry Dressing

6 medium peaches
½ C raw almond butter
1 C sweet cherries, pitted
¼ C vanilla-flavored almond milk
1 T maple syrup
½ t vanilla extract
½ C sliced almonds

Slice peaches longitudinally in ½-inch gores
(about 8), carefully cutting fruit away from pit.
Arrange, pinwheel-fashion, on salad plates.
Combine almond butter, cherries, almond milk,
maple syrup and vanilla in a blender until smooth.
Drizzle dressing over fruit. Top with almonds.

Yield: 6 servings

TASTY TIP::
Substitute
nectarines for
peaches and/or
raspberries for
cherries.

*"Eating a healthy diet is three times more effective
than taking a cholesterol-lowering statin drug
for preventing a recurrent heart attack."*

John Abramson, MD

Pineapple Parfait

3 C fresh pineapple chunks
2 ripe bananas
¾ C coconut milk
¼ C salba, ground
1 T organic raw blue agave nectar
½ t pure almond extract
4 raspberries

Place all ingredients into blender and process just until smooth. Pour into 6-oz parfait glasses and top each with a raspberry. Chill several hours.

Yield: 4 servings

NUTRI-NOTE:
Benefits of coconut milk include anti-viral and anti-carcinogenic properties. Its fats help balance high cholesterol and its antimicrobial properties can heal ulcers in the mouth and in the gastrointestinal tract.

"Eat foods with a high nutritional bang per caloric buck."

Joel Fuhrman, MD

Pistachio Ice Cream

4 large bananas, peeled and frozen
¼ C raw pistachio nuts
½ t stevia powder
¼ t pure vanilla extract
¼ t almond extract

In a food processor, coarsely chop 1/8 C pistachios and set aside. Grind remaining pistachios to a fine powder. Transfer to a bowl and stir in stevia, almond and vanilla extracts. Pass frozen bananas through a Champion juicer using the solid plate. Gently fold in powdered nut mix. Transfer to serving bowls and sprinkle coarsely ground nuts on top. Serve immediately.

Yield: 2 yummy servings

NUTRI-NOTE:
Pistachios are the richest source of potassium of all the nut family; one ounce of pistachios contains a whopping 310 mg. Pistachios are also rich in phytosterols, helpful in lowering cholesterol and fighting cancer.

"The closer food is to its natural, God-created state, the higher its nutritional value."

Dr. Bernard Jensen

Pralines and Cream

2 bananas, peeled, sliced in pennies, and frozen
½ C So Delicious vanilla-flavored coconut milk
2 T raw almond butter
2 T Salba, finely ground in coffee mill
1 t pure maple syrup
½ t vanilla
¼ C hazelnuts
2 pecan halves

Place all ingredients except nuts into blender jar. Puree slowly until creamy. Pour into two dessert bowls. Grind hazelnuts finely in food processor. Transfer into dessert bowls and incorporate gently. Place pecan half atop each bowl and serve.

Yield: 2 servings

NUTRI-NOTE:
Salba (chia seeds), is 20% protein and has more omega-3 fatty acids than any other plant food.

*"A genuine scientific breakthrough...
is the health-giving, disease-preventing power
of a truly healthful eating-style."*

Joel Fuhrman, MD

Raspberry Sorbet

3 large bananas, peeled and frozen
1 ½ C frozen raspberries
1 ½ t stevia powder
2 fresh raspberries
2 fresh mint leaves

Pass 1 frozen banana through a Champion juicer using the solid plate. Pass remaining fruit through the juicer, alternating raspberries and bananas. Add stevia to soft mixture and gently swirl together until color is consistent throughout. Place into serving dishes, top with fresh raspberry, and garnish with mint leaf. Serve immediately.

Yield: 2 servings

NUTRI-NOTE:
The ellagitannin content in raspberries, which the body converts to ellagic acid upon consumption, may have cancer protective value.

"'Food' and 'nutrition' are no longer synonyms."

Victoria Boutenko

JUICES & SMOOTHIES

Blueberry Hemp Smoothie

3 T hempseeds, shelled
1 speckled banana
¼ t vanilla
½ C almond milk
¼ C blueberries

Grind hempseeds for a few seconds in a coffee mill. Place in blender with other ingredients and liquefy. Serve chilled.

Yield: 12 oz.

NUTRI-NOTE:
Hempseeds are 33% protein and very high in omega-3 fatty acids and minerals like magnesium, phosphorus, and zinc.

"In this plate of food, I see the entire universe supporting my existence."

Zen Blessing Before Meals

Cantaloupe Cooler

½ ripe cantaloupe
6 oz vanilla flavored almond milk
¼ t almond extract
3 T hulled hempseeds, ground
5 fresh basil leaves

Cut cantaloupe into thin slices, remove seeds and rind and discard. Cut melon into large chunks. Place all ingredients except 2 basil leaves into blender and liquefy. Pour into serving glasses, chill, and garnish with basil leaf before serving.

Yield: 2 servings

NUTRI-NOTE:
The antioxidants in cantaloupe help fight heart disease, high blood pressure, diabetes, and cancer.

"What you put into your body several times a day, every day, will have far more impact on your well-being than anything else you do."

Joseph Mercola, MD

Carrot Spinach Juice

4 large carrots, scraped and tops removed
¼ lb fresh spinach, washed well
1 Fuji apple, cored and cut into eighths

Alternately pass 1 carrot, 1 wad of spinach, and 1 apple section through juicer until all the produce has been juiced. Chill before serving.

Yield: About 16 oz

TASTY TIP:
Substitute kale for spinach.

"Learn to genuinely appreciate vegetables for what they do for you, and your palate will soon follow suit."

Mark Percival

Goji Berry Smoothie

¼ C soaked goji berries
¼ C blueberries
¼ C dark sweet cherries, pitted
¼ C raspberries
¼ C strawberries, stems removed
2 T salba, ground
½ C unsweetened apple juice

Blend together all ingredients in a blender. Serve chilled.

Yield: 12 oz

NUTRI-NOTE:
Goji berries contain antioxidants that help combat premature aging, with 10 times more antioxidants than red grapes and 10 to 30 times the anthocyanins of red wine.

"The type and quality of the food you eat has a profound influence on your health."

Joseph Mercola, MD

Goji Lemonade

¼ C dried goji berries
6 C filtered water
1 lemon
½ t vanilla extract
2 t organic raw blue agave nectar

Cut lemon crosswise in ¼ inch slices. Place in 2 qt pitcher with all other ingredients. Leave in refrigerator overnight. Strain out berries just before serving and set aside to use in smoothie (see above). Stir lemonade well and serve with lemon slice.

Yield: 6 C

TASTY TIP:
This refreshing drink gets better with age – keep in refrigerator for up to 5 nights.

"Never before has there been such a mountain of empirical research supporting a whole foods, plant-based diet."

T. Colin Campbell, PhD.

It's Easy Being Green Smoothie

1 apple, washed and cored
4 stalks celery
1 ripe avocado
2 C ice water

Chop apple and celery into one inch chunks.
Place into blender. Scoop out avocado and add
to blender. Pour in water slowly and puree until
very smooth.

Yield: 4 C

NUTRI-NOTE:
Most of the fat in an
avocado is
monounsaturated —
the "good" kind that
actually lowers choles-
terol levels.

*"By restoring the electrical potential of the cells,
raw foods rejuvenate the life force
and health of the organism."*

Gabriel Cousens, MD.

Mango Crème Smoothie

1 C frozen mango cubes
½ C almond milk
1 ripe banana
2 T ground flaxseeds
1 C So Delicious vanilla flavored coconut milk
   yogurt
2 t maple syrup

Combine the mango and almond milk in a blender, using the ice crusher function. Add banana, flax, yogurt, and maple syrup. Blend until smooth.

Yield: 16 oz

TASTY TIP:
Papaya may be substituted for mango in a delicious variation of this recipe.

"My illness is due to my doctor's insistence
that I drink milk, a white fluid
they force down helpless babies."

W. C. Fields

Melon Spritzer

2 C ripe honeydew cubes
2 C watermelon cubes
2 C sparkling apple cider
1 t vanilla extract

Pass melon cubes through juicer. Stir in vanilla and apple cider. Serve chilled.

Yield: 6 C

NUTRI-NOTE:
Honeydew is an excellent source of Vitamin C as well as folate, well known for its power to protect against birth defects.

"There is already enough data on the anticancer effects of food for everyone to begin applying this treatment to themselves."

David Servan-Schreiber, MD, PhD

Nut Nog

½ C raw Brazil nuts, soaked overnight
½ C raw hazelnuts, soaked overnight
½ C pitted dates, soaked overnight
1 ½ C water
½ t vanilla
Pinch grated nutmeg

Blend all ingredients except nutmeg at high speed until frothy. Chill about 30 minutes. Stir, sprinkle with nutmeg, and serve.

Yield: 2 ½ C

NUTRI-NOTE:
Soaking and blending makes these nuts a digestible, rich source of protein, selenium and zinc.

"You are what you eat."

American Proverb

Peachy Keen

1 ½ C sliced peaches, fresh or frozen
1 ripe banana
2 T gold flaxseeds, ground
¾ C vanilla flavored almond milk
¼ t almond extract

Thoroughly blend together all ingredients until
smooth.

Yield: 16 oz

NUTRI-NOTE:
Flaxseeds are an
excellent source of
omega-3 immune-
boosting fats, and of
anti-cancer chemicals
called lignans.

*"Chemoprevention by edible phytochemicals
is now considered to be an inexpensive,
readily applicable, acceptable and accessible
approach to cancer control and management."*

Y-J Surh

Pina Colada

1 ½ C fresh pineapple chunks
1 ripe banana
1 C So Delicious vanilla flavored coconut milk
1 T maple syrup
2 T gold flaxseeds, ground
¼ C unsweetened coconut shreds

In a coffee mill, grind coconut into powder. Pour into blender with all of the other ingredients. Blend on low for a few seconds until ingredients are thoroughly incorporated. Then blend at high speed until well pureed.

Yield: 2 C

NUTRI-NOTE:
Pineapple stem and core fruit contain the enzyme bromelain, which offers potential anti-inflammatory and digestive benefits.

*"Tell me what you eat,
and I will tell you what you are."*

G. K. Chesterton

Potassium Juice

1 C fresh parsley
1 C fresh spinach
5 medium carrots, scrubbed
2 stalks celery with leaves

Push all ingredients through juice extractor,
alternating leafy greens with carrots and celery.
Drink at room temperature or slightly chilled.

Yield: 8 oz

NUTRI-NOTE:
Potassium- rich juices
help protect our
bodies against
alzheimer's disease,
arthritis,
atherosclerosis,
cancer and diabetes.

*"People who live solely on fresh raw foods
supplemented with a sufficient volume and variety of
fresh raw vegetable and fruit juices,
do not develop cancers."*

Dr. Norman Walker

Raspberry Almond Smoothie

2/3 C raspberries
1 ripe banana
6 oz unsweetened apple juice
3 T gold flaxseeds, ground
¼ t almond extract

Liquefy all ingredients in blender. Serve chilled.

Yield: 16 oz

TASTY TIP:
For a delicious varia-
tion, use strawberries
or blackberries in
place of all or some of
the raspberries.

*"As far as cancer is concerned,
food trumps contaminants every time."*

T. Colin Campbell, PhD

Salad in a Glass

3 oz arugula, washed and patted dry
10 medium carrots, peeled
1 large beet, peeled

Push all vegetables through a juice extractor, alternating root vegetables and greens. Drink immediately or chill, stir, and consume within a few hours.

Yield: 24 oz.

NUTRI-NOTE:
Raw beets contain high amounts of lycopene, particularly protective against cancers of the prostate, lung, breast and stomach.

"He that eats till he is sick
must fast till he is well."

English Proverb

Strawberry Lemonade

6 small strawberries, trimmed
¼ C fresh lemon juice
¼ t vanilla extract
¾ C cold water
2 T raw organic blue agave nectar

Place all ingredients into a blender and liquefy.
Pour over ice cubes and serve.

Yield: 16 refreshing oz

NUTRI-NOTE:
The USDA Human Nutrition Center on Aging found that strawberries help improve brain function and slow the decline of age-related loss of cognitive and motor skills.

"Every day, at every meal, we can choose food that will defend our bodies against the invasion of cancer."

David Servan-Schreiber, MD, PhD

Strawberry Smoothie

2/3 C strawberries, trimmed
1 ripe banana
6 oz vanilla-flavored almond milk
3 T Salba, ground

Place all ingredients in a blender and combine thoroughly.

Yield: 12 oz

NUTRI-NOTE:
Strawberries are high in vitamin C and valuable against rheumatism, gout, and catarrh.

"We never repent of having eaten too little."

Thomas Jefferson

Tomato Juice

2 medium vine ripened tomatoes
½ medium red bell pepper
½ medium onion
1 clove garlic, diced
½ t sea salt
Dash pepper
½ lemon, cut into wedges

Chop tomatoes, pepper, and onion. Place all ingredients except lemon into blender and liquefy. Chill. Pour into glasses and garnish with lemon wedges.

Yield: 1 ½ C

NUTRI-NOTE:
Raw vegetable cocktails provide a great source of minerals.

"We are all dietetic sinners;
only a small percent of what we eat nourishes us;
the balance goes to waste and loss of energy."

William Osler, MD

Tropical Delight

1 C fresh ripe pineapple chunks
1 ripe banana
1 ripe mango, peeled and sliced
½ C vanilla flavored almond milk
¼ t vanilla extract
½ t organic raw blue agave syrup (optional)

Puree all ingredients together thoroughly in a blender. Serve chilled.

Yield: 16 oz.

"'Real' foods are…more effective than supplements, and they are more effective in combination than when eaten separately."

David Servan-Schreiber, MD, PhD

APPENDICES

Appendix A

Eat Vegan: Disease prevention and longevity

Heart Disease. According to Dr. William Castelli (Framingham Heart Study), Dr. Caldwell Esselstyn (Cleveland Clinic), and Dr. Dean Ornish (Preventive Medicine Research Institute), meat eaters have an increased risk – and vegetarians a significantly lower risk – of heart disease. Animal products such as meat and eggs are the only dietary sources of cholesterol and the chief sources of saturated fat, the main causes of heart disease. Avoiding these foods can reduce the risk of heart attack by up to 90%. The fiber in vegetarian diets not only binds up unneeded cholesterol and plaque-causing agents, but also helps in reversing atherosclerosis (hardening of the arteries). Vegetarians overall are 20% less likely to die from a heart attack than meat-eaters.

Cancer. Animal products are usually high in fat and always devoid of fiber, both of which are risk factors for cancer. A British study of over 6000 vegetarians found them 40% less likely to die of cancer than meat-eaters. One of the most dramatic findings of the China Project was the strong association between foods of animal origin and cancer. In a striking experiment, a diet high in animal protein was fed to animals with rapidly growing liver cancer; when animal protein was replaced with plant protein, the tumors stopped growing.

Breast and prostate cancer risk is associated with high animal protein and fat. Over two decades of research at the Loma Linda University in California reveals that men who eat meat are three times more likely to suffer from prostate cancer than vegetarians. According to a study done by the National Cancer Research Institute of Tokyo, vegetarianism reduces the risk of breast cancer in women by 25%. Japanese women who followed a western style meat-based diet were eight times more likely to develop breast cancer than Japanese women who followed a more traditional plant-based diet.

Similarly, in a study of over 35,000 American women, those who developed non-Hodgkins lymphoma had higher intakes of animal fat, especially from red meat.

Fiber intake is a critical factor in the prevention of cancer, especially of the colon. In a University of Hawaii study, vegetarians, on average, ate almost twice as much fiber as meat eaters. Vegetarians are therefore much less likely to suffer from constipation than meat-eaters. The *Journal of the National Cancer Institute* reported back in the 1970's that there is not a single population in the world with a high meat intake which does not have a high rate of colon cancer. Dr. Dennis Burkitt declared, "small stools, large hospitals."

In addition to fiber, of all the natural cancer prevention substances discovered, none has been found to be animal derived. Cancer-protective phytonutrients like sulforofane, indoles, carotenoids, lycopene, lignans, lentinan, triterpenoids, chlorophyll, catechins – to name a few out of 30,000 -- are only available in plant-based diets. Blood analysis of vegetarians also reveals that they have higher levels of specialized white cells which attack and kill cancer cells than do non-vegetarians.

Diabetes. Diabetes, especially type 2 adult-onset diabetes, is also rampant among animal-eaters. In a 21-year study of over 27,000 Seventh Day Adventists, the death rate due to diabetes was found to be only 45% that of the general population. A vegan diet can actually reverse mature-onset diabetes. When the diet recommended by the American Diabetes Association (ADA) and a vegan diet were compared over a 12 week period, the vegan group lost an average of 16 pounds while the ADA group lost eight pounds; furthermore, the ADA group needed as much medication as before, while the vegan group needed considerably less. The *American Journal of Clinical Nutrition* described a study in which researchers put diabetics on a vegetarian diet; 45% of the patients were able to discontinue their insulin injections.

Obesity. Study after study shows that vegetarians are less likely to be overweight than meat eaters. One study found that vegans weighed an average of 10 pounds less than the rest of the population. Another study suggested they weighed 30 pounds less, and a third found that vegetarians had 30% less body fat than non-vegetarians. A study which increased fruit and vegetable consumption by only four servings per day resulted in 24% lower risk of obesity. Obesity is, of course, a risk factor for serious disease. According to Daniel Monti, MD, Director of the Center of Integrative Medicine at Thomas Jefferson University, too much body fat shortens life and lessens life quality, increasing the likelihood of developing, or dying of, heart disease, stroke, diabetes, high blood pressure, asthma, cancer, osteoarthritis, and gallbladder disease.

Kidney and Gall Stones. Diets high in animal protein can cause the body to excrete more calcium, oxalate and uric acid, which form into kidney and gallbladder stones. Vegetarian diets have been shown to reduce the chance of forming these stones. An ultrasound study found that 18% of meat-eating women had symptomless gallstones, compared with only 10% in vegetarians.

Osteoporosis. Because an acidic diet rich in animal products pulls alkaline mineral buffers out of the bones, vegetarians are at a lower risk for osteoporosis (weakening of the bones). Countries that consume the lowest amounts of dairy products have correspondingly low levels of osteoporosis, and conversely those which consume the highest amounts of dairy products have the highest levels of osteoporosis.

Pulmonary Disease. A large study of 43,000 men published in the medical journal *Thorax* revealed that the plant-rich Mediterranean Diet cut the risk of chronic obstructive pulmonary disease (COPD) by 50%. Vegetarianism can also benefit those already diagnosed with lung diseases like bronchitis and asthma. A 1985 year-long study conducted by the University Hospital in Linkoping, Sweden, showed that over 90% of bronchial asthma patients had less severe and less frequent attacks and reduced need for medication while eating a vegetarian diet.

Multiple sclerosis (MS). Dr. Roy Swank of the Montreal Neurological Institute followed 144 MS patients for over 30 years; he found only five percent deaths among the low saturated animal fat diet group as compared with 80 percent deaths in the high saturated fat diet. New international studies show a strong link between cow's milk and MS. According to Dr. William Castelli, a switch to a vegetarian diet could help more than 90% of all MS victims arrest the disease process and improve their condition.

Appendix B

Eat Vegan: Reduction of toxins and contaminants

Livestock drugs. There are over 20,000 different drugs, including steroids, antibiotics, growth hormones and other veterinary drugs that are given to livestock animals. These drugs are taken into the human body when animal foods are consumed.

Hormones. Factory farm livestock are fed vast amounts of synthetic hormones, like Bovine Growth Hormone. These additives cause precocious sexuality, weight gain, cancer, and other health disturbances in meat eaters. In Puerto Rico, some children have matured sexually as early as four to eight years old as a result of exposure to livestock hormones. Young teenage boys developed full breasts, but when their exposure to hormone-treated meat and dairy products ended, their symptoms receded.

In the United States, dangerous growth hormones are found in practically every feedlot in the country. The fattening hormone DES (Di-Ethyl Stilbestrol), though banned, is still in use by factory farmers. This hormone is so potent that workers who absorbed even minute amounts of it developed symptoms of impotence, infertility, enlarged and tender breasts, and changes in their voice register. Even one molecule of DES is sufficient to trigger cancer. Yet several years after its ban, the FDA found that 500,000 cattle had been illegally implanted with DES!

Pesticides and other agricultural poisons.
Animal foods contain far higher concentrations of
agricultural chemicals than plant foods,
including pesticides and herbicides. Flesh
products are the most concentrated source of
pesticides in the human diet. Ninety-five to
ninety-nine percent of toxic chemical residues in
the American diet come from meat, fish, dairy
products, and eggs. Pesticides such as dioxin (a
component of Agent Orange), heptachlor, PCB's,
DDT, and Aldrin are so toxic that even the most
minute doses cause miscarriages, birth defects,
cancer, and death in lab animals. The fat-soluble
pesticides become concentrated in the fatty flesh
of the animals, ensuring a plentiful supply of
poison in the diet of meat-eaters.

Chemical Additives. Animal flesh naturally
turns a sickly gray-green color soon after it is
slaughtered. The meat industry hides this
discoloration and keeps the meat blood red by
adding nitrates and other preservatives. These
preservatives are so toxic that cancer researcher
Dr. William Lijinsky says, "I don't even feed
nitrate-laden foods to my cat." Farmed salmon is
usually treated with artificial colors made with
carcinogenic dyes.

Pathogenic Microorganisms. There are a
host of bacteria and viruses, some quite
dangerous, that are common to animals. Micro-
organisms are present in plant foods too, but
their number and danger to human health are by
no means comparable to those in meat. Dr.
Richard Novick of the Public Health Institute
reported to Congress, "The meat we buy is grossly

contaminated with both coliform bacteria and salmonella." Over 4,000,000 cases of salmonella poisoning occur annually, causing nausea, diarrhea, abdominal cramps, fever, vomiting, chills, and even death. The abuse of antibiotics in factory farms has led to salmonella strains which are resistant not only to antibiotics, but even to cooking.

Parasites. Toxoplasmosis contaminates eighty-five percent of all pig products; the *trichinella spiralis* worm is found in many species of carnivores and omnivores; and tapeworms and many other parasites are contracted from eating meat.

Appendix C

Eat Raw: The health hazards of microwaving

As noted in "Comparative Study of Food Prepared Conventionally and in the Microwave Oven" (*Raum & Zelt* 1992):

"A basic hypothesis of natural medicine states that the introduction into the human body of molecules and energies to which it is not accustomed is much more likely to cause harm than good. Micro-waved food contains both molecules and energies not present in food cooked in the way humans have been cooking food since the discovery of fire. Microwave energy from the sun and other stars is direct current based. Artificially produced microwaves, including those in ovens, are produced from alternating current and force a billion or more polarity reversals per second in every food molecule they hit. Production of unnatural molecules is inevitable."

As noted in the Russian investigations published by the Atlantis Rising Educational Center in Portland, Oregon, microwave exposure at levels considered acceptable for normal ingestion produced effects noted by both German and Russian researchers in three categories: destruction of nutrients in foods, cancer-causing effects, and biological effects of exposure.

Microwaving was shown to cause significant decreases (60% to 90%) in the nutritional value of all foods tested by the Russian researchers. The following are the most important findings:

- Decreased bioavailability [capability of the body to utilize nutrients] of B-complex vitamins, vitamin C, vitamin E, and essential minerals
- Destruction of the nutritive value of nucleoproteins in meats
- A marked acceleration of structural disintegration in all foods
- Alteration of the body's ability to break down plant alkaloids [organic nitrogen based elements] when raw, cooked, or frozen vegetables were exposed to microwaves for even extremely short durations
- General disorders in digestive system function caused by unstable breakdown of foods subjected to microwaves

Carcinogens were formed in virtually all foods tested.

- Microwaving prepared meats sufficiently to insure sanitary ingestion caused formation of nitrosamines, well-known carcinogens.

- Microwaving milk and cereal grains converted some amino acids into cancer-causing agents.

- Extremely short exposure of raw, cooked, or frozen vegetables — especially root vegetables — converted their plant alkaloids into carcinogenic free radicals (highly reactive incomplete molecules.)

Among the other noted cancer-causing effects of microwaving were:

- Creation of a "binding effect" to radioactivity in the atmosphere, thus causing a marked increase in the amount of radioactive particle saturation in foods
- Malfunctions within the lymphatic system and degeneration of the immune potential of the body to protect against certain forms of malignancies
- A higher percentage than normal of cancerous cells within the blood serum and of tumors such as sarcomas
- Damage to cancer protective plant substances, such as nitrilosides
- Stomach and intestinal cancerous growths

REFERENCES

Alexander J, "Chemical and biological properties related to toxicity of heated fats," *Environmental Health* 7(1):125-38 (January 1981)

Assembly of Life Sciences, *Diet, Nutrition, and Cancer,* National Research Council, 1982

Bjerregaard p, Jorgensen M, Borch-Johnsen K, "Serum lipids of Greenland Inuit in relation to Inuit genetic heritage, western-isation and migration,"*Atherosclerosis* 174 (2004) 391–398

Bon Appetit, Sept. 2002

Boutenko, Victoria, *12 Steps to Raw Foods,* Berkeley: North Atlantic, 2007

Bowman, Pam, *Cooking in the Raw,* Brookhaven, PA: TLC, 2004

Brookes Graham and Peter Barfoot, of PG Economics Ltd., UK, in their report, *GM Crops: The Global Economic and Environmental Impact-The First Nine Years 1996-2004*

The Cancer Project, www.Cancerproject.org, *The Survivor's Handbook: Eating Right for Cancer Survival*

Campbell, T. Colin, *The China Project,* Ithaca: Paracelsian, 1996

Campbell, T. Colin, *The China Study,* Dallas: Benbella, 2006

Cobb, Brenda, "It's cool to eat raw," *Healthkeepers Magazine* 26:14, October 2010

Cohen, Kim, *Raw to Radiant,* Aspen, CO: Radiant Health, 2006

Cooking Light, June 2002

Cordain, Loren, *The Paleo Diet,* Hoboken, NJ: John Wiley and Sons, 2002

Cousens, Gabriel, *Conscious Eating*, Berkeley: North Atlantic, 2000

Esselstyn, Rip, *Engine 2 Diet: The Texas Firefighter's 28-Day Save-Your-Life Plan That Lowers Cholesterol and Burns Away the Pounds*, Wellness, 2009

Fallon, Sally, *Nourishing Traditions*, San Diego, ProMotion, 1995

Fuhrman, Joel, *Eat for Health*, Gift of Health, 2008

Fuhrman, Joel, *Eat to Live*, Littleton, CO: PSG, 1981

Goldberg T et al, "Advanced glycation end products in commonly consumed foods," *American Dietetic Association Journal* 105(4):647 (April 2005)

Haas, Elson, *Staying Healthy with the Seasons*, Celestial Arts, 2004

Hayford, Kelly, *If It's Not Food...Don't Eat It!*, Boulder, CO; Delphic Corner, 2005

Howell, Edward Howell, *Enzyme Nutrition: The Food Enzyme Concept*, 1985

http://altmedicine.about.com/od/popularhealthdiets/a/Raw_Food.htm

http://www.bodyincredible.com/the-importance-of-seasonal-eating/

http://deliciouslivingmag.com/health/nutrition/3-25-guide-to-seasonal-eating/

http://en.wikipedia.org/wiki/Genetically_modified_food

http://en.wikipedia.org/wiki/Natural_foods

http://en.wikipedia.org/wiki/Paleolithic_diet

http://en.wikipedia.org/wiki/Veganism

http://environment.about.com/od/greenlivingdesign/a/
locally_grown.htm

http://kankyoinstitute.lit.konanu.ac.jp/~taniguchi/archives/
monkey_c.pdf

http://vegetarian.about.com/od/glossary/g/Vegan.htm

http://www.bodyincredible.com/the-importance-of-seasonal-eating

http://www.britishmeat.com/49.htm

http://Drmirkin.com/nutrition/

http://www.greenpeace.org/international/en/press/releases/gmo-
papaya-scandal-in-thailand

http://www.naturalnews.com/029724_sugar_beets_lawsuit.html

http://www.nk.rim.or.jp/~fumiaki/eng/Deform.html (2/2)2007/02/
09 23:32:47

http://www.organicconsumers.org/biod/papaya090804.cfm

http://www.ecomall.com/greenshopping/pveg1.htm

http://www.nk.rim.or.jp/~fumiaki/eng/Deform.html (1/2)2007/02/
09 23:32:47

http://www.suite101.com/content/the-facts-about-cottonseed-oil-
a213236#ixzz14YY06zmb. "The facts about cottonseed oil: this
ingredient on grocer's shelves could harm your health"

http://www.thebestofrawfood.com/

http://www.vegan-nutritionista.com/

International Service for the Acquisition of Agri-biotech Applications, "Virus-resistant gm squash more vulnerable to bacterial wilt attack, study finds," *Crop Biotech Update*, Oct. 30, 2009

International Vegetarian Union, www.ivu.org/recipes
Katz, David, *The Way to Eat*, Sourcebooks, Naperville, IL, 2002

Light, Dawn, *Dawn of a New Day Raw Dessert* E-Book www.dawn ofaNewDay.com

Link L and Potter J, "Diseases associated with raw versus cooked vegetables and cancer risk," Cancer Epidemiology *Biomarkers and Prevention*13(9):1422-35 (Sept. 2004)

LocalHarvest.org, LocalHarvest Newsletter, February 24, 2009

Mercola, Dr. Joseph, *Dr. Mercola's Total Health Cookbook & Program*, Chicago, 2003, mercola.com

Mulvad G and Pedersen HS, " Orsoq: Eat meat and blubber from sea mammals and avoid cardiovascular disease," Inuit Whaling, Inuit Circumpolar Conference, June 1992

Pitchford, Paul, *Healing with Whole Foods: Asian Traditions and Modern Nutrition*, Trade, 2002

Pollan, Michael, *In Defense of Food: An Eater's Manifesto*, New York: Penguin, 2008

Price, Weston, *Nutrition and Physical Degeneration*, La Mesa, CA: Price-Pottenger Nutrition Foundation, 1945

Reno, Tosca,*The Eat-Clean Diet Cookbook*, Toronto: Robert Kennedy, Mississauga, ON, 2007

Schmid, Ronald, *Traditional Foods are Your Best Medicine*, Stratford, CT, Ocean View: 1987

Silberstein, Susan, *Hungry for Health,* Conshohocken, PA: Infinity, 2005

Servan-Schreiber, David, *Anticancer,* NY: Viking Penguin, 2009

Smith, Jeffrey M. "Doctors and animals alike tell us: avoid genetically modified food," *Healing Our World,* Hippocrates Health Institute 30 (2), 20

Smith, Jeffrey M. *Genetic Roulette: The Documented Health Risks of Genetically Engineered Foods,* Chelsea Green: 2007

Sparandeo, James, *The Immune System Enhancement Diet,* 1993

Swedish National Food Administration, "Acrylamide in heat-processed foods," Livsmedelsverket, Stockholm, April 2002

Turner, Kristina, *Self-Healing Cookbook: A Macrobiotic Primer for Healing Body, Mind and Moods With Whole, Natural Foods,* Earthtones, 2002

Vallejo Tomas-Barberan, and Garcia Viguera, "Phenolic compound contents in edible parts of broccoli inflorescences after domestic cooking," *The Journal of the Science of Food and Agriculture* (November 2003, Vol. 83, issue 14, pp. 1511-1516)

Vegetarian Resource Group, http://www.vrg.org/nutrition/protein.htm

Walters, Terry, *Clean Food,* Sterling Epicure, 2009

Wayne, Anthony and Lawrence Newell, "The Hidden Hazards of Microwave Cooking," *Immune Perspectives* XI(3), fall 2007:6-13

Wigmore, Ann, *The Wheatgrass Book,* Wayne, NJ: Avery, 1985

Wood, Rebecca *The New Whole Foods Encyclopedia,* Penguin, 2010

www.Allrecipes.com

www.Catherinerudat.com Get Fit Newsletter

www.Chow.com/recipes

www.GMO Africa.org

www.GreensonaBudget.org

www.HappyCow.net/recipes

www.NativeFoods.com

www.PlanetVeggie.com

www.RealSimple.com/food-recipes

www.RethinkingCancer.org

www.Vegetarian.about.com

www.TheVeggieTable.com

www.VegWeb.com

www.WholeFoodsMarket.com/recipes

RECIPE INDEX

Index

C

D

K

White Bean Dip with Cucumber 101
Wraps, Collard 88

Y

Yogurt with Blueberries 102

Z

Zucchini
  Apple Pancakes 175
  Garbanzo Tacos 103
  Spaghetti and Sauce 176

For more information or to order additional copies,
contact

Center for Advancement in Cancer Education
130 Almshouse Road #107A
Richboro, PA 18954
www.BeatCancer.org
info@BeatCancer.org
888-551-2223

Proceeds from the sale of this book
benefit the cancer prevention programs of

BeatCancer.org
Center for Advancement in Cancer Education

CPSIA information can be obtained at www.ICGtesting.com
Printed in the USA
BVOW11s1937200815

414111BV00003B/4/P